They Lost More Than They Took.

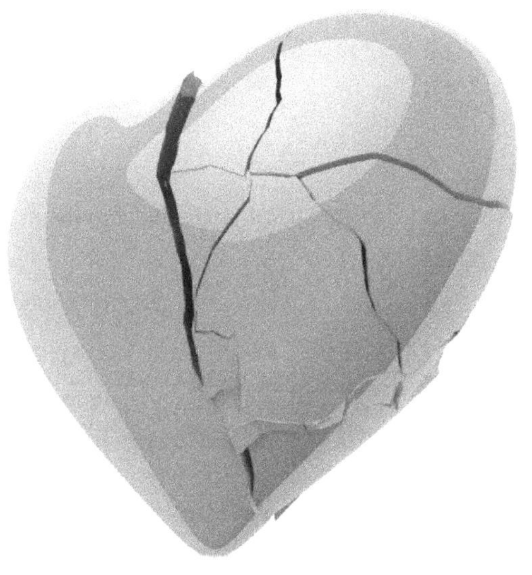

Ty Redden

They Lost More Than They Took

Author Ty Redden

Paperback 978-1-7368788-2-8

Cover design: Danielle Ferreira

Published by: Caged Bird Publishing

www.cagedbirdpublishing.com

DEDICATION

My Aunt Channy was the inspiration for writing this book. She was honest, loving, spiritual and ready for whatever.
I miss her beyond words my Angel in heaven I want to make her proud.
~ RIP Aunt Channy.

CONTENTS

ACKNOWLEDGMENTS

My Son, Ty'Jhamere King Ackridge, who has pushed me to be a better person. The person who has given me unconditional love. My real-life Superman. Having you in my life is like heaven on earth. My only goal is to make you proud of me.

Shout to my mother, Clydette Redden, my #1 Supporter. You have always been a great mother/best friend. Seeing you work hard and never giving up or complaining showed me nothing but strength. I admire you in ways you may not even understand. I will forever take good care of you. Love, your Mazda.

Papi, Carlos Redden, I'm grateful that we can go to each other and be our true, authentic, and genuine selves with one another. You have always been a shoulder to lean on and I know that I can always count on you. I love you!

Zafir Redden, not only my photographer, but someone who saw my dream and wanted to be a part of making it come true. I love you beyond words.

Thank you, my Goose, someone I love dearly my heartbeat. You always loved me unconditionally no matter right or wrong. Your love is guaranteed to stay the same. I love you.

Thank you, Markeeta Brown, my sister for always listening and giving a shoulder when I need it and letting me know that anything is possible. You believed in me when I did not believe in myself.

Thank you to my little sister, Chiriga Howie, for encouraging me and praying for me. One of my best supporters. She's someone who has never judged or belittled me even at my worst. Throughout the good and bad circumstances, we have shared, she shows up for me every time.

My sister, Regina LeCompte, who has always been by my side through thick and thin your support and love means so much to me.

I want to give a shoutout to my god sister, Cheri Wilson, who has been my rider through thick and thin. We have cried and laughed together and she has always been my number one protector. I love her to the moon and back.

My Life Coach, Ariel Harper. Thank you for never giving up on me through my struggles, insecurities, and lack of self-love. Thank you for encouraging me and helping me see my self-worth so that I can be a better person. Thank you for taking the time to help me accomplish one of my many goals. I thank God for placing a genuine person in my life. I love you.

Thanks to all my family and friends who have loved and supported me through my struggles and life lessons. I appreciate everyone.

1 CHAPTER

The Girl With The Big Heart

Well, let me introduce myself to everyone outside of the author bio on the back of the book. I'm Ty; short for "that's none of your business." Sike. That's just what everybody calls me. If you know me, then you know I love to dance, and I love to watch movies. I love old movies, too, like the Mannequin, Teen Witch, A Long Kiss Goodnight, Love Jones just to name a few. My favorite shows are Family Matters, Martin, and Golden Girls, and I love RnB music. When I am riding around in my car, I sing like it is nobody's business because, hey, it isn't. My favorite colors are grey and pink. I love to read books to expand my knowledge and I love to travel.

I've always been a private person and I never really shared what I have gone through with many people. So, this book is going to be shocking to many because they never really knew all that I have endured in my life regarding my relationships over the past twenty years. I believe that my friends will be the most shocked because they were around when everything was happening, but I never spoke about it. I just went through it, especially the abuse. The cheating was done publicly, so there was no point in keeping that under wraps.

In this book, I share a lot of my struggles; but before we get into the down and dirty, I want you to know that I *love* my family. I am family-oriented, and we are remarkably close knit. We throw gatherings, family reunions, etc. Aunts are like mother figures and uncles are like father figures. Cousins call each other brother and sister because we all grew up together.

My favorite boy cousin, whose name is Dee, and my favorite girl cousin is also named Dee. How crazy is that? If you ever see me at a family function, then you know that Dee, female cousin, is not far behind. Our family members used to always say that whenever we were together, it was always going to be trouble. We were basically inseparable, whenever we would leave each other from causing "trouble," she always made sure that she told me that she loved me.

My brothers and I have a great relationship. I'm like their security guard and vice versa. My little brother, Ziare, is my protector. He acts like he is the big brother even though I am older. Whenever we link up, it is always a good time. We can talk about any and everything. As his sister, I am glad that he feels comfortable enough to talk to me about different things; it means a lot to me.

Once, Ziare, and I were at my Goose's house, and he set a blanket on fire. And my Goose snapped! And as his older sister, I took the blame for him. She wanted to hit me but did not because deep down inside she knew that it was not me. So, I did not get into trouble, but I did have to take the cuss out for him; he would've gotten the switch off the tree. Needless to say, I basically saved his whole life that day.

Now my other brother, Curtis, and I, spend a lot of time together; we have a special and unbreakable bond. I take him *real* personal. Our relationship is a little different than my other brother. I don't know if he was trying to toughen me up or what when we were younger, but we really went through it. Curtis was always trying to fight. He has cut my hair, cut my finger with a knife, just ignorant to his sister. It is crazy because we are literally thick as thieves, but he is my everything.

My sisters on the other hand; I have too many to count. It is a whole bunch of us. My younger sister, Renee, is near and dear to my heart. She has been there for me throughout some of my toughest times over the years and we have been each other's support system as we have shared similar life experiences. I have always taken pride in the bond that we have because she has consistently been a listening ear in my time of need and a pure heart if in need of prayer. I can go to her with just about anything and she is never judgmental. Growing up, her Mom took me in as her own, frequently having sleepovers at her house; we spent a lot of time together. We shared a sense of style and love for music and too many other similarities to list.

I remember riding around in Renee's hooptie when we were 16, blasting Peedie Crack "Ring the Alarm" and taking turns singing verses to our favorite songs. We used to go on double dates and trips out of the country; we were always on the same wave. One thing about Renee is when it comes down to it, she likes to be the life of the party just like me. With all the siblings that I have, it has never been "half-brother" or "half-sister." It is always "brother and sister." Even the siblings that my biological brothers and sisters have were still my family, too. Simply out, we are all family. Three of my aunts moved to Atlanta when I was younger, and I would visit them frequently. There's Aunt Ree, Aunt Channy, Aunt Angel. Whenever I am with them, I always have the best time. We would go out to sing, go to the movies, talk trash; it is just a different vibe with them. One aunt would always want me to sing and dance. Another would want me to be really prissy with my hair and nails done. And my other aunt, Aunt Channy, was a mixture of the two.

She had no filter on her mouth. It was what it was. She did not care who liked it and would stand up for whoever, plus herself. She has even stood up for me a couple times. There was a time I told her about these girls that were picking on me at school. I told her that I did not have any problems fighting them; I just didn't want to get jumped. So, when I came out of school the next day, guess who was sitting there, waiting for the girls? Yep. Aunt. Channy. I love her with all my heart and soul. She would always say, "I love you to the moon and back."

Unfortunately, during the process of writing this book, my Aunt Channy passed away. With such an already close-knit family, we have drawn closer and leaned on each other than ever before. You never know how much you really need family. I needed my family more than they needed me. My aunt left behind three kids and three grandchildren. They are my little cousins, but they are more like sisters. Aunt Channy called me her daughter, and she always told everybody that she had four, not just three. They call me every day, they like to talk to me on the phone, and they want to do things with me. I feel as though I have a big responsibility to fulfill and I am willing to uphold that. I am not the type of person who will make promises I can't keep.

As much as her passing has pained me, I still have the memories to keep me going. Thanksgiving was one of her favorite holidays. We would always go to my Goose's house, sing karaoke, watch movies, play games while everybody is preparing and cooking. I would peel and cut the sweet potatoes, rinse off the greens, etc. Everybody had their own specific job. Christmas was also one of her favorite holidays; she made sure she got everybody a present. It could have just been a sock in a bag, a lotion, or anything else. That is what she loved to do.

My family is the life of the party and I think that is where I get my love for dancing from. And where do I dance? Two words. House. Parties. Back in the day, many people knew me as the girl that always had the best house parties. The thing is that my mom would work from 3-11pm as a nurse, so I would invite everybody from my side of town to come over to my house and just dance. No smoking. No drinking. Just dancing. Just how I liked it. And it was not just the dancing that I loved as a young girl; I simply loved music. And I especially loved me some Kriss Kross. You know, “Kriss Kross’ll make ya Jump, jump!” And the light-skinned one? Daddy Mac? Oh, my goodness! He was my favorite. I loved him so much that I manifested my son to look just like him. I used to tell everybody that I would have a son that would be light-skinned and have long hair just like Daddy Mac. And guess what? I did! Crazy, right? You will learn more about my son a little later.

I was so in love with Kriss Kross that one time, my Aunt Ree flew me all the way to Atlanta to meet Kriss Kross in person. However, the trip did not turn out how I had planned. I ended up losing all my luggage, all of my clothes, shoes, everything. My Aunt Ree had to buy me a whole new wardrobe. But all that did not matter because once I met my real-life celebrity crush, all of my worries and stress went out the window. On top of meeting them, they signed a t-shirt and a book bag just for little ole 'me. It was one of the best experiences of my life!

Music was my outlet, so I guess those house parties were one of the reasons why my house was the hangout spot. At my house, it was just me and my mom. We had the best relationship. However, she would get on my nerves, just like all moms do, but I loved her to the fullest.

One of my sisters, Rina, would come to stay with us from time to time. A month here. A month there. When she would stay, we would dress alike, go skating every Friday at Elsmere, and she would do my hair in these crazy styles just like the girls in the music videos: SWV, 702, TLC, etc. with a bang here, a knot here, just craziness. If you have a sister, then you know that a sister isn't a sister if y'all don't fight. She would lock me in the bedroom, put her fists up, and make me fight her. I guess she thought I was too nice and needed me to grow some thick skin.

The thing was, she was right; I needed some thicker skin. I created a bad habit of adopting people. It was just something that was innate in me. It could have been a friend's cousin, a friend, a friend's sister. Whoever! I never wanted anybody to feel the way I felt when it came to friendships and relationships, so I would adopt people. I believe that this toxic trait started with my first relationship a man, my father.

I was only about five years old when my dad was sentenced to six years in jail. I would visit him and write him letters. We stayed in contact as much as we could. But we had an inconsistent relationship because he was in and out of jail while I was growing up. So, we didn't fully establish a father-daughter bond until I was around twenty-six years old with a child on my hip. Although we began to build and work on our relationship, I became envious of the bond that he had created with my son. The bond that he should have had with me. He would do all these things for his grandson: call him on the phone, pick him up from daycare to hang out, visit him; just gave him the whole world. Everything that a father should have done for his daughter.

But as time went on, after praying and finally making amends in my heart, I was able to move past those feelings and enjoy the time and the memories that I am currently creating with him and my son. I can now say that my dad and I have a decent relationship. I genuinely love him, and I refuse to make the same mistakes that he made with me, by truly being intentional in the role that I have in my son's life.

But because of the tainted and skewed relationship I had with my father, I had internally and subconsciously vowed that no one else that I encountered would feel the same way that I did. It was easy to do, especially since my house was the hot spot. My mom always had snacks at our house, and I always had nice clothes. So, my friends would come over, wear my clothes, spend the night, etc.

I had so many "friends" because I have always been the type of person to be there. If a friend needed something, I was there. If they needed food, I would get them lunch or at least share with them what I had. If they needed clothes, I would make sure that they had something to put on. I even had friends that would run away to my house and I would take them in under my roof.

The crazy thing is that even with all the "friends" around me, I was the only one giving the compliments. I was the only one motivating and encouraging, but not uplifting my own self when I needed it the most. It did not make sense to me and it still doesn't, but just making someone else feel good made me feel good. With all the friend-adopting that I did, I had a small circle of people that

I would call my true friends. One of them, whom I call my god sister, Chelsey, did not like the fact that I had all of these people that I had adopted as "friends." She did not like that I was taking people in under my wing.

Now Chelsey is the kind of friend that is outspoken and does not hold her tongue. She has no filter just like my Aunt Channy. She will fight any and everybody. When we were younger, she would get upset with me if she saw that I was with a new person or friend, or even an old friend. She was very protective of me. She would ask me who they were and what I was doing for them. Like, third degree investigations. She just wanted me to stop overextending myself to strangers and would literally not talk to me for days because she would get that bothered by it. I mean, what can I say? I love helping people.

Helping people was my drug. Material things did not make me feel good, unless it came to one thing. That one thing was...you ready? Teddy bears! Yes! I used to have, like a thousand bears on my bed. You can just never go wrong with a fluffy teddy bear. I loved teddy bears so much that one time I got into a fight with one of my friends. Like a crazy fight because she was being really rough with one of my bears. Nope. I was not having that! If nobody were giving me hugs and love, I knew that my teddy bears would.

My older sister, Mona, did not like me adopting friends either; she was the complete opposite of me. She kept her circle as tight as a cheerio when it came to friendship. I called her the good troll, and I was the bad troll. I admired her strength because she did not take any shit from anyone. Mona did not tolerate cheating or abuse in her relationships. She set boundaries with the men she was involved with, friends that she kept close, and she honored those boundaries. If you ever crossed the line with Mona, she did not give you the opportunity to do it again! If you struck out once with her, you only got one strike… and you were out!

Me on the other hand, I did not have the same backbone as Mona when it came to relationships. Although I had the same set of friends since I was thirteen years old, I always seemed to find new people to "adopt". I did not listen when Chelsey would warn me about always allowing new people to get close to me nor did I follow in Mona's footsteps. As time went on and I grew older, I continued to surround myself with more new faces, "adopting" this one and that one; not seeing how one day a kind heart might catch up to me...let alone bite me in the ass. I never listened but I wish I had; I guess you can say I am hardheaded. I am now learning the scars I've gained over the years are really just tally marks of everything I've been through.

I have always been that person who wanted people to love me like I loved them. Just reciprocate the love that I have poured out. But when the love is unrequited, it can be draining. I am constantly pouring love into your cup, but nobody is there to pour love back into mine. I had to realize that nobody owes me anything. If someone does not love me, oh well. If someone does not care for me, oh well. I had to learn this in the most difficult ways that I have ever experienced, and I'm sharing this with you so that you don't have to go down the same pathway as I did to get to true self-esteem and self-worth in order to feel loved

2 CHAPTER

My Very First Love

I was at the ripe young age of eighteen years old when I fell in love and had my first boyfriend, Lawrence. I can remember the very first day that I met him like it was yesterday. I was working at McDonald's at the time, my very first job. He came in one day with some of his friends. And with me being a rookie and all, I spilled something all over the floor. Man! With his slick mouth, he says, "Next time, you can pour it on me." And it was a wrap from there. We exchanged numbers and began to talk on the phone every single day. After about a good five months, we finally connected in person and began to hang out; I was a beginner at the whole dating thing.

After some time passed, we finally made it official as an item. We would do little things that couples usually do in a relationship: go out to eat, sit and talk, etc. I would buy him little things. You know, something light like boxers or socks. It could not be anything big because mind you, I was eighteen and worked at McDonalds. However, he was my first real grown-up relationship, and not to add, he was four years older than me.

I have always had a thing for older men. They just seem to treat you better in my opinion or so I thought. I truly felt like a grown ass woman. I was eighteen, I had a job, my own car, was ready to get my first apartment, in addition, I had just enrolled for classes at Delaware Technical Community College for Medical Assistance, and do not forget, I had a man. I was living my best life. And it was the best, in the beginning.

Lawrence was a nice dude; I met his family and became close with his siblings, but with the siblings came drama, especially with his sisters. One of his sisters, Mina, in the beginning was friendly, cool to be around, and knew how to have a good time. She would hang out with me, take me places, and even introduce me to others as Lawrence's girlfriend. After awhile, her invitations to hang out didn't excite me anymore because she began to extend those invitations to old flings or other women that wanted to be next in line for Lawrence. Whenever Mina would get mad at me for whatever reason, she would call over those girls for a sleepover. They would get all dressed up, call each other, "Sis", watch movies, etc., just to piss me off. She would also try to hook Lawrence up with other girls knowing that we were together. One time, she even tried to hook him up with one of my cousins, Daisy. She did not know that it was my cousin, but that's not the point. The point is that she would do this stupid stuff just to hurt me.

Lawrence valued Mina's opinion about women and the kicker is that Lawrence loved all of this attention. He loved going over to Mina's house because he had the F word. Not that word; get your head out of the gutter. He had *freedom*. Mina was always gonna be down for her brother; she was always going to put him first above anyone else. And once I realized that, that "Sis" stuff got played out real quick. I came to the conclusion that Mina wasn't my sister at all; she was his and his alone.

Mina not only looked out for her brother, but she also made sure that she benefited from all the females that were around and wanted to be with Lawerence. She would also use all of us to her advantage. One girl would do this favor for her, the other would buy this for her, I would do something else for her, etc. She would play us against each other because she knew that we needed to be on her good side since she had a special bond with her brother. If she were mad at you, she would use her brother against you. But to be honest, I think he was scared of her. Scared of his sister?! Yes!

He would never stand up to his sister or stand up for me for that matter. Since she was one of the major reasons why he behaved the way he did, he probably wanted to say something, but never did. Regardless of the strife between us, I became close with his sisters. I would let Lawrence's sisters and girl cousins come over to my house and raid my closet. When I would go out, I would buy them stuff here and there. Just doing the most.

There I go, thinking that I must take care of other people, again.

Another sister in particular, Mya, was older and would tell me that her brother was not really ready to be in a serious relationship. She would even go so far as to tell me that he had some major growing up to do. She had been hurt before and could see the signs and she didn't want me to experience what she had gone through. Despite her warnings, I continued to date him. Not listening to her warnings caused me so much pain and heartache. I told ya'll I can be hardheaded at times.

Even Lawrence's best friend, Nay, tried to me warn me as well. Nay was chill and I could see why they were best friends. One time, she snapped on Mina and asked her, "Why do you always have these extra females around? Like for what?" Mina's house was never empty. Whether it was the Fourth of July, Thanksgiving, Easter, Hanukkah you name it! It was bound to be some females there. As hardheaded as I was, Nay still warned me about being with Lawrence even if that was her best friend.

There was one time when Mina met a guy who also had a sister that just so happened to be attracted to my man, Lawrence. It wasn't blatant and in my face flirting, but I just felt something in my being telling me that something wasn't right. Again, I tried to brush it off and not think negatively about the person I was in love with. But as time went on, and she continued to throw herself onto my boyfriend, he decided to call her bluff.

One night, he told me not to come by his mom's house because he said he was tired. I was fine with it, but Mya, the one I was close with, asked me to come over, not knowing that something suspicious was going on with her brother. She gets there and calls me, but by the time she does, I was already over there, literally catching him having sex with Mina's boyfriend's sister in the bed!

I could not believe my eyes! For the first time ever in my life, I grabbed him and slapped the crap out of him and left out of that house so fast! The next thing I knew, I hear Mina say, "Get her! Get her!" I turned around and three people started to jump me. I fought back as much as I could and got away. Thank God that I didn't have any bad scars or permanent damage.

I went home and did not call a soul. Not one cousin, a brother, or a sister. I did not want to involve anyone as bad as that may sound because I knew that I wasn't done dealing with him.

When Nay heard about them jumping me, she was pissed. I guess they were bragging about what happened, especially about the part me finding him in the bed with another girl. She came to visit me the next day and advised me again to be careful. She wanted me to truly understand that Lawrence's sister was not my family, so I wouldn't play myself.

Mya continued to try to warn me about Lawrence, but after staying with him and watching her brother continue to cheat on me, she just let me live my life how I wanted to. You may be wondering, "Why didn't you listen, Ty?" The simple answer is I was young and in love. And at eighteen years old, you think you know everything, but you don't.

He continued to cheat on me with numerous women and one of them happened to be one of Mina's friends, Shanice, whom I had become real friendly with. We were the type of friends that had each other back, especially when it came to Lawrence and the other females that he was messing with. She would snap more than I would. I thought that she was really riding for me, until I realized she really wasn't.

I ended up letting her stay with me in my first apartment while she got herself on her feet. There I go adopting people, again. You'll probably hear me say that a lot throughout the book.

So, you might as well get used to it now. But trust me, there's purpose even in that.

After staying with me for a little while, I noticed that she and Lawrence started acting strange around each other when we would all hang out. They both were being too friendly with each other. And to find out, they were sleeping together. Even though I was hurt, I forgave him and we continued our relationship for two more years after that. We began to have more serious conversation and started talking about getting married and having children together. The whole nine yards. And as much sex as we were having, I never ended up pregnant. So, I came to the conclusion, at twenty years old, that I couldn't have children. But to my surprise, we ended up having a baby! Sorry, I mean, he ended up having a baby with a girl that he had a one-night stand with.

Let me set the scene for you. Boomp!

I went to visit him at Mina's house and I am steadily knocking on the door, but he would not let me in. He says that he is busy, but I'm hearing a female's voice in the background. Turns out that the voice I heard was the girl that he ended up having a baby with. But what will probably surprise you the most is that I stayed with him even after all of that. I was there when she would drop off her baby. I would literally sit there and watch while people would hold his baby and take pictures with his baby. I would even go as far as buying things for the baby as if at twenty years old, I had no more life to live. As if I wasn't worthy enough to have someone not cheat on me. As if I wasn't worthy enough to have someone love me the way I deserved to be loved. This is what I had settled for.

Even after that, he continued with his cheating, and even began to abuse me physically and verbally. He was the first guy to ever hit me, sadly he would not be the last. I didn't tell anybody about the abuse that I was suffering from. I didn't even tell my good friend, Kenya, about it. There was one time where I had made plans with Kenya to just hang out, chill, cook, and just be low-key. That's the type of vibes that we had. Prior to meeting up with her, I caught my boyfriend cheating on me with some girl in a car and whenever I caught my boyfriend cheating, I would never fight the women. I would always stick it to my boyfriend.

Like how can I be angry with the other women that he was cheating on me with? He was the one that owed me the loyalty, not them! Who's to say that they didn't feel the exact same way I did? Who's to say that they didn't smile when his phone number came through their phone when he called?

After catching him and arguing with him, he turned his aggression on me. I tried to run away from him, and he chased me down. He got on top of me, grabbed me by the neck and choked me; I was trying to push him off me as hard as I could. I ended up having all these bleeding scratches on my neck. He had really dug his fingers into my skin like it was nobody's business.

I ended up going over to Kenya's house with these scratches because I had already told her that I would, however I did try to hide my wounds. But it was no use; she saw the scratches. She literally just sat there, hugged me, and cried. She didn't say anything. She didn't ask what happened. She kind of just figured it out on her own. I told her that I was ready to get out. After all the black eyes, after all the bruises, after all the fist fighting and cheating, I was at my wits end and I wanted out.

As I reflect on the relationship that I had with Lawrence, I can sincerely say that it wasn't all bad times. Lawrence and I had some fun times as well. At the tender age of eighteen, he taught me some life lessons. He introduced me to different things that I carry with me to this very day. And to be honest, there is no bad blood between Shanice and I, the one that I let live in my house. The friend that went behind my back and started messing with Lawrence. Matter of fact now that I think about it...sike! It's still all love. And some people even think that I am crazy for not feeling any disdain towards her, and I'll let you know why. It's because when you know what type of relationship that a person is getting into because you've been in a relationship with that person, you have nothing, and I mean *nothing*, to be envious or jealous of. Because if he, did it to me, he'll do it to you.

Before we officially broke up, Lawrence cried to me one day, which took me by surprise. Like, really? *You're* crying?! He always had this hard demeanor. He told me that he loved me enough to tell me to stop taking him back because he was no good for me. He wished that he would have treated me better. He wished he had another chance to make it right. Up until this day, Lawrence still tells me whenever he sees me that he wished that he would have married me. He even dedicated *We Belong Together* by Mariah Carey to me to express how he truly felt. He apologizes for all that he did and acknowledges that he had a lot of maturing to do when it came to relationships. He tells me that I am a good woman, and any man would be happy to be with me, and he hopes that I find true love because he knows that I deserve nothing, but the best.

He also tells me to let him know if I need him for anything, which is crazy because he was the one that did me wrong. He hurt me, but he doesn't want anybody else to hurt me like he did. I never really understood the concept of that, but I guess he saw his wrong doings and regretted it.

At eighteen, you think you know everything, and you think you know what you want. After being in that relationship, I was able to discern more and more, and learn some valuable life lessons to keep in my back pocket. One major life lesson that I learned was that I knew what I didn't want to go through anymore. I knew what I wanted, but everything doesn't always happen the way we want it to. Now does it?

3 CHAPTER

Strike Two

When I decided to remove myself from a tumultuous relationship, I was in full blown recovery mode. I wasn't looking to jump right back into any kind of relationship; I was focusing on finding myself. During this time of self-reflection, my sister, Mona, had another baby, my youngest niece, and I decided to move in with her and help her out with her newborn. While staying with my sister for about five months, my niece's grandmother and uncle came into town to visit. But in the midst of their visit, I began a relationship with her uncle. Now it wasn't an immediate relationship because remember I was still trying to recuperate from the last one.

So let me set the scene. Boomp!

I remember it like it was yesterday. I was in the kitchen cooking and cleaning, and the uncle came in and slipped me his number. Yup. Real smooth with it. I was surprised because I wasn't even looking really cute that day. I had on a t-shirt and some sweatpants, something real simple and laidback. Not even dressed up and this man gives me his number. But I guess it's true what Drake says,

"*Sweatpants, hair tied, chillin' with no make-up on;*

That's when you're the prettiest,

I hope that you don't take it wrong."

So, I took the number, but didn't even bother to call him, text him, or anything. I told y'all that I was working on me, myself, and I, and I wasn't really feeling anybody or thinking about dating at the time.

A few weeks went by and he came back around. We were laughing and joking. You know, the heehee-ing and haha-ing. He was throwing little hints out, but I wasn't picking up what he was putting down because I simply didn't want to. A few weeks after that, I decided to send him a little text and from there we became friends. For three months, we texted. We talked. We hung out a couple of times. He even changed his name in my phone to "My Baby" and would dedicate love songs to me which I thought was cute.

When my car broke down, he would give me rides to work. Upon picking me up, he literally brought me roses every single day for thirty days straight. He would bring me and Mona breakfast from time to time. So, I started to let him hang out with me at my place with Kenya and Curtis, and about a month later, we decided to take it to the next level. He bought me a car and we made it official as a couple!

To me, he was just different; he gave different vibes, and I was digging it. The conversations that we would have, the friendship that blossomed had me thinking that I had caught me a *real* man, and I couldn't pass this up. We would go to church every Sunday and created this undeniable bond with each other. A bond that even my family could see.

Curtis used to always be over my house and would stay over from time to time. But once I got into a relationship, the dynamics changed a bit, and I had to adjust that. When I finally let him stay the night with me for the first time, the next morning I went to work, came back home, and saw 6 bags in my house. Like 6 bags. I immediately thought it was my brother. So I busted through on his Nextel. Chirp! Chirp! "Curtis! Sister or not, you are not about to move up in my house!" He hit me back. Chirp! " It wasn't me, Ty, it was ole' boy!" Haha! This man just moved his stuff right on in; made himself real comfortable. This was a whole arrangement that I was one, not expecting and two, foreign to me. He was the first man I had ever lived with. He had me cooking, running his bath water, etc. And I didn't mind. I was so head over hills with him; I didn't even care to look at another man. I SWEAR I WAS PREPARED TO GO A LIFETIME WITH THIS MAN!

He had me reciprocating everything he was putting down this time around. I would do little nice things for him; "just because" gifts. Just because I was that much in love with him. One year for his birthday, I coordinated a little gathering for him with his close friends and family. Although it was small, I went all out with the food, drinks, even bought him a nice outfit to make sure that he had a wonderful time. I even became attached with his cousins girlfriends, and thank God it didn't come with drama like the last relationship.

But before we go on, let me just give you a quick breakdown of where we are in my relationship journey. As you know, I was in a relationship with my first boyfriend, Lawrence, from ages eighteen to twenty, and then ended up with a second guy who is the dude that you are currently reading about. By the way, spoiler alert! He ends up being my son’s father. We continued a relationship until I was about thirty-one. And the relationship moved fast, but it didn't *move fast,* if that makes sense. If it doesn’t, it will.

I was able to meet his mom and his two children. I automatically had the philosophy that when you are with someone, you two share the load. When you are with someone, you don't get to choose what parts of the relationship you want and don't want to be a part of. So, I immediately started taking care of his kids like they were mine and be around him and his family more often. Sounds familiar, right? You know what else sounds familiar? Cheating and abuse.

My son's father was a cheater. He was also physically, mentally, verbally, and emotionally abusive towards me. Even with the abuse and the multiple relationships, in 2007, we still planned to get married. As much of a surprise it may be, I was in a good space and I was at an age where I was so ready to get married. I knew I was ready because when my father had my sister by another woman, my sister's mom called my mom and told her that she had a baby with my dad. So, my mom did what any sane woman would do, and she knocked him upside the head with a vase, and she never looked back.

From that point on, I never saw my mom with a lot of men. She never had a lot of guys in and out of the house, all the way up until I was twenty-four years old. I've only seen her with one or two guys, and that's it. She was settled. And that's how I felt about my son's father. I was settled. I did not need to mess with a whole lot of men. I was settled with him, for him, and I fought for him.

We got engaged and I had organized everything for our wedding. I had my bridesmaids in place with their dresses, the venue, my dress, the rings, the limo, everything. We even moved into a different house. But unbeknownst to me, there was a female neighbor from our old neighborhood who already knew my fiancé, and they had reconnected on a more intimate level. Her name was Jasmine.

It's crazy how I found out about Jasmine. The thing is that I wasn't even looking for anything. The evidence just happened to fall in my lap. I was cleaning one day and found some photos and some letters. In the letter, Jasmine writes about how she loves him, and how she still wants to be with him even though she knew that we were engaged. Yup. That's right. She knew about me. She knew who I was and had even spoken to me a few times. But by this point, she didn't care. She was in love with him, but so was I.

One time during our engagement, I was taking a shower, and I took my ring off and placed it in a particular spot. But when I returned, it had been moved. Now, I thought I was crazy, but I came to find out, he had taken the ring that he had proposed to me with, took a picture of it and sent it to Jasmine asking her, "Yes or no?" The au-da-ci-ty!

I actually caught him cheating on me with Jasmine. I went to visit him at a trap house, and the lady there must not have realized what was going on and what was about to go down; so, she let me in. I walked to the room where I knew he would be, but the door was closed and locked. I stopped and listened, and I could hear voices and movement. So, you know what I did? I did what any other pissed off woman would do. I banged on the door. BANG! BANG! BANG. Immediately, the voices stopped. Everything was quiet. And it continued to be quiet.

So, I just left the house. As I am getting into my car, he throws me against the wall of a house and screams, "DON'T CHECK IN ON ME! I'M A GROWN MAN! YOU'RE NOT MY PROBATION OFFICER!" I snatched away, pulled off in my car, and called Donna. You will learn more about her later. I went to her house and just sat there and cried on her shoulder. The next day, I went to my Aunt Mee-Mee's house, who was my caterer for the wedding. At that point, I was done with the wedding. I was crushed and hurt as we sat and talked. While talking, guess who pops up crying and pleading, but as far as I was concerned, the wedding was over.

Not only was he cheating on me with Jasmine, but a whole slew of women. The women he had cheated on me with were so caught up and in love with this man because he had pulled so much wool over their eyes, it was ridiculous. He had gone as far as taking pictures of my dog, showing it to other women, telling them that he had just purchased it for them, and to pick out a nickname for the dog. He would go apartment hunting with them, and have these women think that they were going to move in together. He even met their parents and everything. There were women who said that they had been together for two years, three years, five years, etc. It was mind blowing.

There was one woman who found me on social media, Fatima; she happened to be my neighbor in a previous neighborhood that I used to reside in. She would like my pictures from time to time on Facebook, but then out of the blue, she messaged me, told me to give her a call, and during our phone conversation, she disclosed to me that she had been messing around with my man.

Once, he called me and cussed me all the way out. He thought I was messing with this guy; the irony and the audacity! He mentioned the guy's name and everything. I had no idea who this man was, but the name did ring a bell with me. It sounded familiar because that was Fatima's boyfriend's name.

So, let's set the scene. Boomp!

The mix up happened because he was hanging out with his boys and he had one, too many drinks; he was a lightweight. Couldn't hold any type of liquor. So, he called me, trying to angrily ask me about Fatima's boyfriend, then he got silent and hung up. He ended up apologizing to me, and even though I knew the truth; I didn't say anything. I just enjoyed the apology. I had ultimately stopped confronting him about the cheating because it would result in me getting busted up in my face or dragged out of the house. So hey, I deserved that, plus more!

One of my little cousins, Alicia, who used to live with me, knew Fatima personally, and didn't tell me about it. Come to find out, Alicia was spending time with this girl over at her house, then come back and bust it up with me like nothing was happening. So, I confronted Alicia about it, and she said that since she saw him doing what he wanted, she thought that we were no longer in a relationship. Plus, she didn't want to hurt my feelings, and was hoping that I would just move on one day, but I didn't.

Another time, he was driving around with Jasmine, rode past another girl, Deja, and she decided to jump in front of the car. They start fighting and he kicks Deja's teeth out. He gets locked up, and who does he decide to call to bail him out? You know it! Me. And guess who sat in court with him for assault charges? Me.

There was another woman that came out of the woodworks, who called me when he had gotten locked up again and asked me to contribute to his bail money! Just craziness! But the crazier thing is that I had tolerated so much with this man that this was just the norm for me. People thought that because I had dealt with so much of his nonsense in the past that he could continue to take advantagc of me, and I let him.

My sister, Mona, had a baby by my son's father's brother, so his brother and I were already well acquainted with each other. He had even witnessed things that I had experienced with my first boyfriend, Lawrence. So, when he found out that I was messing with his brother, he told Mona to tell me that I should be careful. Nobody knows you better than your own brother.

Speaking of Lawrence, there was a time when he and my son's father had almost gotten into it.

So let me set the scene. Boomp!

We all used to hang out on this one side of town, and one of the neighbors was Hispanic, Ms. J.; her and her daughters were so cool to be around, and we became friendly with one another. Ms. J. would play music and cook all the time, and created a warm vibe in the neighborhood. One day, my son's father and I began to argue while I was over there, and Lawrence, whose sister, Mina, lived on the same block as Ms. J, saw us arguing and ran up to defend me. And you know what he said to me, again? He told me that he had already hurt me enough and he would never let anybody else hurt me like he did, even my son's father. My son's father didn't admit and say this to me until later in life.

I'm ashamed to say that even though my son's father physically abused me, I still fought for him. Once, I was hanging out with my son's father and his cousin, Angie. His cousin was always so encouraging, supportive and just cool and down to earth. She would tell me that I was crazy, but that she had loved me ever since the day we met, and I felt the exact same way about her. We all went out to eat, and afterwards, we went back to my son's father's uncle's house where there was a lot of drug trafficking. And everybody knew that if you were selling drugs, that you do not sit on the step.

So, when we pulled up, there was this guy who was trying to sell drugs, sitting on my son's father's uncle's step. So, my son's father started snapping and making a big deal about it. He told the guy to move, and the guy responded and said he would move when he was ready to move. They started arguing and getting into each other's face; it started to get intense.

Now mind you, we had just gone out to eat and had a great time. My son's father is a light drinker, only had a Corona, so he was a little tipsy. The guy tried to swing on my son's father, but instead I saw that he wasn't in the best condition to fight, so I decided to ride for the team and swing on the guy myself. The drug dealer was surprised that it was me and just left. Thank God that it didn't turn out differently, but I was going to hold us down whenever it was necessary.

Our relationship had its up and downs, but it wasn't all bad. Some of the good things was that we had some pretty good times together. We had similar interests which made us really good friends. We would get couples 'pictures to commemorate our relationship back when K-Mart was poppin'. We would go out and ride up to Philly and go shopping, sit back, chill, go to the park, watch movies, crack jokes, and just be us. Just like me, he loved to dance, too. When we would hang out, we would dance all night long, but he would make sure to keep me close by, especially depending on the scenery. For holidays and birthdays, he would get me little things and ask me what I would want. It wasn't always a surprise because he wanted to make sure that he got the perfect gift for me. Sometimes, he would take the initiative to surprise me, but most of the time, he just got what I asked for which was fine with me. It's the thought that counts, right?

When we were at odds and have our downs, he would make it up to me by writing me love letters, play *They Don't Know* x Jon B, and take me on rides and have a date night. He had a sensitive side and knew just what to do to win me back.

I remember, whenever my son's father and I would go to the movies, get dressed up for date night, ride to Philly, or whatever it was, I was always ready. Ready for what? Ready for whatever. Ready for something to come up because he just cheated so much. I wouldn't speak things into existence, but I'm a pretty smart cookie. I would put the pieces together, like one plus one equals two and two plus two equals four? Nine times out of ten, I was usually right with my predictions. So, I would always find out what he was doing. So, I always had to be on my P's and Q's.

Somewhere along the way, I knew I lost myself, again. I had to have lost it because what woman in their right mind would tolerate the disrespect that I was dealing with? Could love really have me this blind that it would allow me to tolerate someone cheating on me with woman after woman? After all the cheating, I would still take him back, time after time again.

Princess Jasmine

Jasmine was a young girl who lived with her mom and didn't have a car. She had gone off to Job Corps, which was about an hour and a half away, so my son's father wasn't able to see his young tenderoni as often as he liked. So, one time he decided to go down and visit her, and during his visit, called me to come get him and told me this bold-faced lie that he went to see his cousin, and his cousin's car broke down. I, still lost in my self-worth, went to go get him.

Since Jasmine didn't have a car, she literally called me on my birthday and asked me if I could pick him up from jail. My son's father was locked up and having a ride home was the only way that he could be released. But here is the kicker; she wanted me to drop him off to her. Whew, chileee!

Jasmine was special to my son's father, but a thorn in my side. Since he did not work, he had a lot of spare time during the day to do his dirt. They would hang out, go on dates, chill at her mom's house, even go up to Philly together, etc. It was like he was in a whole other relationship. Once, I called him and I guess he was already on the phone with Jasmine. So, when he switched over all I could hear him saying was, "I've been thinking about you and I miss you, Jasmine." Blah, blah, blah, blah. Telling her all these sweet nothings, but the whole time he was talking to me, sending me paragraphs via text intended for her and didn't even know it. Just stupid.

I decided one day that I wanted to visit her so that we could talk face to face, woman to woman. I wanted to look into the eyes of the woman that my man was cheating on me with. When we sat down to talk, she told me how she ended up having an abortion with his baby and how he had written love letters to her as well. She was so excited to tell me all the things that he bought for her, what songs they had sex to, how he would pamper her, etc. When she told me that, a piece of me just died. She was rubbing it all in my face. Digging her thorn deeper and deeper.

I started to think about all the moments that we had shared together, in and out of the bedroom, the fact that we were trying to have a baby ourselves, etc. Hurt is an understatement. I was crushed to my core, so you know what I did? I listened to music. I told y'all I love me some RnB. You know it's something about the right song that will just capture exactly how you feel. Monica's CD, The Makings of Me, was on repeat. Ring the Alarm Beyonce, on repeat. and Love by Keyshia Cole, on repeat.

> *"I used to think that I wasn't fine enough*
> *And I used to think that I wasn't wild enough*
> *But I won't waste my time tryna figure out why you playin' games*
> *What's this all about?*
> *And I can't believe*
> *You're hurting me*
> *I met your girl, what a difference*
> *What you see in her*
> *You ain't seen in me*
> *But I guess it was all just make believe"*

WHY HER?!

But you know what, I didn't stay there. I knew I had to end things with him. After wallowing in my feelings, I had to pick myself up and get back on the horse. Even though, I had removed him from my life, he continued to indirectly pop up back in my life.

My guy cousin, Dee, was dating this girl, Nina, and they had a baby together. He and his girlfriend invited me to their Sip n ' See. For those who don't know, a Sip n 'See is where you have family and friends come over to 'sip 'on whatever your drink of choice is and 'see 'the baby that has just been born. So, I went to the gathering, met Nina, and we hit it off. She was really cool. We're all eating, drinking, having a good time. So here I am enjoying myself and here comes Jasmine's sister walking into the party. Little did I know that her sister was really good friends with my Nina, Dee's girlfriend. So, without trying to cause too much attention to myself, I continue to sit there and scope the scene.

Her sister and I exchange some words. She proceeds to tell me that her sister, Jasmine, is messing around with my son's father off and on, and I just say, "Okay." Never asked any other questions like, "How long? Are they still messing around?" because it is what it is, and I wasn't going to let her know that she had ruffled my feathers or had an upper hand on me. So, I kept my cool. Now while we are exchanging words, some more people come to the party. And one of those people is another woman that my son's father had been cheating on me with.

Now this woman I found out about also via Facebook. She would like and comment all of his posts and pictures. Just always doing the most. So, I put two and two together. So, here I am at this party sitting around with the sister of a woman that he was cheating on me with and another woman that he was cheating on me with. But what is crazy is that, at that time, they didn't even know what was going on, but I knew. I continued to keep my composure, have a good time, crack jokes, etc.

After the party, I found out that they had all gone on a trip together, and in the midst of their conversations, the Facebook girl mentioned her dude's name, and Jasmine's sister recognized the name, and that's when everything came out about what was really going on. The gag is that I didn't have to say anything. Your dirty work will always come to light.

The Turning Point

On top of dealing with Jasmine, I also had to deal with my son's father's children's mother. A lot of unnecessary drama came with that, too. She would do and say petty stuff just to piss me off. She would call me and brag that he was just over her house. She would say that he would never leave her alone. Regardless, I still cared for his kids and took care of them like they were our own children. I would make sure that they were good.

My sister Mona worked at Children's Place, so I would always get a banging discount and rack up on so many clothes for them. I would take them shopping, throw them birthday parties and slumber parties, take his daughter to get her hair and feet done, etc. People thought that his daughter was mine, I was that invested. She came to live with us for a couple months, and I even began to call her my daughter. Even though he treated me like crap, I still made sure that his kids were straight.

That's just the type of person I am. A few years later, after having my own child, his children's mother and I eventually started to get along. We, now, have mature conversations and have mutual respect for one another; there's no bad blood which I am grateful for.

Throughout the years, I thought seeing how my son's father treated me and other women was enough for me to keep me on my toes, as much as I tried to stay on top of things, it wasn't. On top of that, it didn't help that his mom would defend him in many situations. She would tell me, "If things fall in your lap, you don't have to react to them" or "If you go looking for something, that's when you will find it." But the thing is, I wasn't looking. He was just moving how he was moving. One thing about my son's father is that he was intelligent, a smooth talker, and a big manipulator. Even after all the wrong that he was doing, he would convince, not just me, but other people, too, that he was not wrong, even his own mother.

But little did she know, she was going to experience the exact same pain I had been experiencing all these years. My son's father's mother ended up having something dropped in her lap about her own marriage. She started to put pieces together and found out that her husband was cheating. His mom called me one day and apologized to me. She said that in the midst of her venting to her son about her own relationship and trying to get some answers on why her man would do her like this after she had been a good woman to him, a light bulb went off in her head. She asked herself, "How can I sit up here and talk to my son about what's going on with me, when he treats women the exact same way?" At that moment, my eyes filled with tears. Something had clicked within her. Now that she was in my situation, she got it. And you know what? I didn't try to rub it in her face. I didn't try to ask questions. All I did was tell her that everything was going to be okay.

And I knew that everything would be okay. I never had to get my son's father back for how he treated me. I never had to seek revenge or payback. I never laughed, when I could've, when he was going through his own struggles. I didn't have to do any of that. The best revenge for me was moving on and moving forward with my life. The healing that took place within me was my revenge.

This might sound crazy, but when my son's father used to cheat on me with Jasmine, I would have these crazy thoughts that they would end up being together, have a family together, have this great big ole 'house up on the hill, etc. The whole shebang! But now that I look back at it, that wasn't something that I should've been worrying about. Because at the end of the day, it didn't even happen.

After him and Jasmine ended things, I remember him making a Facebook post apologizing to me saying, "What comes around goes around," and karma this and karma that. To his surprise, the exact same thing that he did to me, all the cheating he did, Jasmine, ended up doing the exact same thing to him. I guess karma is what they say, a bitch.

I did go back to my son's father from time to time. You know how that goes. We would mess around here and there, but nothing too serious. During our brief time back together, I had some pit bulls, and I remember he would tell me that he thought I loved my dogs more than I loved him. My dogs adored me and protected me. They were my best friends. Once, my son's father started yelling and hollering and got in my face. My dog saw it, started growling at him and was ready to attack! My son's father had to fight the dog off with a broom and accidentally hit himself in the eye with it. I had to rush him to the hospital so he could get some stitches.

While I was in that hospital room, I started to think about all the abuse I had endured. I recognized that I didn't even love him the same way anymore. I started to *hate* him. Just the thought of him made me sick because it was that much damage done. When you no longer care about the person you are dealing with, that is a sign, and that's how I started to feel.

I used to think that my son's father and I would be together forever. I was ready to get married, have a house, the whole shebang, but it didn't work out that way. And as I continued to reflect, I thought about how he really had these women thinking that it was only them. It was such an embarrassment for me. I would think about him and the other women that he had been with and wonder if they were doing the same things that we did. It came to a point that the sex wasn't even exciting anymore. I would lay there afterwards pondering, "Do they do this? Ugh!" It just didn't feel the same anymore.

After a while, I got tired of running myself crazy in my mind. This was something that I didn't want to continue doing. My heart was tired, hurt, and finished. It couldn't take anymore. At some point, you do grow, you change, you get to sit and think and reflect. The reason why I say that they lost more than they took was because after all the taking and taking from me, they lost me. Losing all the genuine love, my presence, my loyalty is enough for you to be on the short end of the stick without me even doing anything in return.

I knew that I wasn't going to be able to totally relinquish myself from my son's father on my own: I wasn't that strong. I knew I needed supernatural. My Goose has been going to her home church for about one thousand years. No, literally. A thousand years. At two o'clock in the morning to be exact, I went to her church steps and sat down in the middle of a thunderstorm for about twenty minutes. I sat in the pouring rain, praying and crying, just asking God to remove my son's father from my life completely. I was at a point where I was tired of hurting. I was tired of the pain and I no longer wanted to accept and tolerate what he was giving me. And God did end up removing him from my life for about three and a half years.

With him no longer in my life, I was in such a good space. A girlfriend of mine, Donna, told me something that I will never forget. She told me that whenever I was with my son's father, I always did good, but when I separated myself from him, when I was by myself, I started doing phenomenal. And that always stuck in my head. So, I continued to be phenomenal.

While working on being a phenomenal woman, there were times that I had relapsed and went back to him. And during those times, I was never able to go full term with a pregnancy. I had two miscarriages back-to-back. Remember, I had already told myself that I couldn't have any children back when I was eighteen. After my self-diagnosis, my doctor confirmed that I couldn't have any children; however, I didn't let that stop me. So, I began to look into adoption.

I desired to have a child so badly, and it didn't help that all my friends and sisters had children already. I was always around children or taking care of someone else's child, and I felt like it was time for me to have my own.

While I was working at a day-care, there was a little girl, whom I had nicknamed Muffin. She was absolutely gorgeous, and

I knew that I wanted to adopt her. Muffin's grandmother had custody of her. We would always speak when she would pick her up and drop her off, and we began to build a cordial relationship. Muffin's parents didn't want to be in her life, her grandmother was getting older, and it was getting harder to take care of her on her own. So we started the conversation of me adopting her. I began to spend more and more time with Muffin at her home, so that we could become comfortable with one another as we continued to look into the process.

After a few months of spending time with Muffin, I ended up getting real sick. I was vomiting and my stomach was cramping, and in the back of my mind I'm thinking the worst. This was the last thing that I needed. So, on May 9th, 2008 at 10 pm, I found out I was pregnant.

4 CHAPTER

King

Once I found out I was pregnant, something just clicked in me. I knew this was my miracle baby that I had prayed for and that I had to protect him at all costs. So, I disappeared. I vanished. I just wanted some peace. And I knew that if I stayed around my son's father, I wasn't going to get that. This was already a high-risk pregnancy which I had to take medication for. So, I didn't care who he decided to be with. He could have been with ten different women, and I did not care. All I cared about was having a healthy pregnancy and a healthy baby boy. I went to stay with my Aunt Channy for the duration of my term.

I would get sick in the shower and throw up, which lasted for the first five months of my pregnancy. But I had great people around me. Living with my aunt and being pregnant was so much fun. We would literally stay up until five in the morning talking, eating, etc. She would make me my favorite pancakes and muffins: blueberry. And she knew exactly how I liked them too, nice, and dark. I would eat twelve blueberry muffins with some orange juice every single night. My cravings were simple: Buffalo wings with ranch dip and 'Now and Later', the candy.

Of course, I would still see my son's father from time to time. But the person that I didn't see was Muffin. I ended up not adopting her because I couldn't keep up with our visits with my pregnancy being high risk and all. I would keep my son's father in the loop when I had my doctor's appointments, but I kept the conversations short. I wasn't going to allow him to prevent or disrupt the very thing that I had been wanting for years because of his foolishness.

But as time went on, I thought it would be good for us to spend some time together because I was getting closer to my due date. When I was about seven months pregnant, we began to see each other more often, but why did I do that? Even at seven months pregnant, he was still putting me through the nonsense. It was around his birthday, and he took my car and disappeared. I figured he went to do him, like he usually does. I found out that he took my car and went to Jasmine's house. Surprise, surprise! Y'all remember Jasmine, right? The girl I called my wedding off for. Now, this wasn't just one time that he did this. This happened multiple times.

He would drop me off at my doctor's appointment and I was calling him constantly to come pick me up. No answer. I was tired of the shenanigans. I called my little sister, Pookie, to pick me up. Now Pookie is my rider. She will handle you without me even being there. She is the epitome of someone who has your back. I had given her a spare key to my car, and we drove to Jasmine's mom's house. And lo and behold, my car was sitting around the corner from her house. He would park around the corner and then walk to her house, I guess trying to be incognito. We ended up pulling off with my car and leaving him stranded there because she didn't have a car, either. Oh, well! Bye!

And hello to my son, King! On January 3rd, 2009, I ended up having a healthy baby boy who was seven pounds and six ounces at 3:39 pm. I had to get an emergency C-section since I had lost a lot of fluid and there was a fifty percent chance that I or my son would survive. Thank God that we both did because that boy is my heart walking around in human form. He is absolutely my everything. And I call him my miracle baby. I am surprised that I didn't end up naming him Miracle.

King's siblings were very much involved in his life as much as possible. I would allow his sister to stay over at my house and she would help a lot with King when he was first born, by feeding him and changing his diaper. She was a great big sister. As she continued to get older, she wanted to do her own thing. Her brother, on the other hand, was very low maintenance. He never really asked for anything; he just wanted to be around me, especially when King was born.

Now, I caused some strife within this blended family dynamics because there were times when their father would tell me not to give them things, and I would do it anyway. But his daughter played her father as well. With all the women that he would mess around with, she was able to hang with them and reap the benefits and perks from these other women because they were in a relationship with her dad. Her brother, on the other hand, was very particular about who he decided to hang around. Most times it was me.

At one point in time, his children were requesting for me to be in their life even after I had moved on from their father. They would tell me that even if I found a new boyfriend, they still wanted to be around me. They loved me and vice versa, and they just wanted me to be happy. And it wasn't just them, his family members too. They all wanted me to be happy. They wanted me to move on and be in a better relationship, but I had to do it on my own terms.

King's dad and I stayed together for a couple of years after he was born, but I realized that I needed to distance myself from him. My son's father wanted to come around more often and try to work things out. I had told myself that I thought it would be good for my son, but not necessarily for me or my heart. When we would argue, I would tell him that he had to leave. I was tired of going through the same thing over and over and would tell him that we were officially over. He would bring up King; he said he would take my son and move out of the state with his mom. He knew how to push my buttons just right. And that just confirmed that if I went back into a relationship with him, it wouldn't be healthy; and if I am in an unhealthy and toxic space, what am I really doing for my son? So I decided to never go back.

At this time, it was just me, my mom, and King. My mom loves King just as much as I do. She went over and beyond for me and her grandson. She stopped working for a whole year, came to live with us, and took care of King while I was at work. Even though it was just us three, I made sure that my son knew that he was loved. I loved up on my son so much that people would call him a mama's boy. I didn't allow him to stay with anybody, but me and my mom. He had too always be with me and up under me.

I remember, once, I went out, which I normally don't do, but I went out for like two hours, and I allowed King to stay with my god sister, Chelsey. When I returned, I banged on the door all loud, and here she comes telling me that he was upset and crying, and she had finally got him to go to sleep. I told her that I cannot go to sleep without my son, and she cussed me all the way out. Hey, what can I tell you? I love my son. I *need* him.

I did the best job that I could and continue to do the best job that I can in raising my son, and to give him experiences in life. You always want to create a better lifestyle for them. You don't want them to miss out on any opportunities that they can have. For my son's first birthday party, everybody thought I was crazy; I had a moon bounce, popcorn machine, cotton candy. I rented a hall and I had it filled with different activities for the guests. I love to create memories. I've taken him to Disney World, Sea World, Nickelodeon Resort, Coco Keys, the Bahamas, just to name a few.

I don’t know how to swim, but my son swims like a fish.

His grandmother lives out of state and we went to visit her a couple of times. While visiting, we would always go to the beach and go swimming, and he thought it was the best vacation ever. I knew that I had to get him swimming lessons for any trips that we took after that. When I was living in an apartment, there was a Dominican lady who was a lifeguard. I asked her if she could teach King how to swim and said she would. When she saw him during that first session, she thought that he was Dominican, Spanish, mixed with something. And I told her, “Nope! He’s light skin with green eyes, but that’s all Black, baby!”

After that first session with her, she decided not to charge me for the lesson, and taught him for free, which was a blessing. King was only five years old and was diving, and here I am a grown woman, and I can't even swim.

Since I didn't know how to swim, I decided to surprise him one good time by taking swimming lessons. Before we went to Sea World, I took about three lessons. All I wanted to do was at least be able to stand in the water, if nothing else, because I was scared to even do that! He was so surprised when I stepped into that water. He ran over to me and gave me the biggest hug ever. I literally had tears in my eyes. I didn't want him to see me crying, so I splashed the water in my face to hide the tears, but he had this grown woman crying. They were happy tears because I saw that me conquering my fears made him smile.

On top of not liking the water, I am not a person that likes rides either; but when I took my son to Universal Studios, I had to become the big kid for him. That was the only way that he was going to have fun. It was around Christmas time and we took so many pictures, watched fireworks, and saw all the characters. The only thing that I could not do and wasn't able to risk was me getting in that water. So again, I just put my feet in, It was the world to him.

I try to love him so much that if nobody else loves him, he knows his mother loves him. Every year, we take two trips, no matter what it is. We've gone to the Poconos to an indoor water park, and we always do a date night. We get dressed up and step out into the bright lights. Sometimes, date night is in the house. We will cook a meal together, watch a movie, etc. I try to do a lot with him because it's just me raising him and with my work schedule, I make sure that he gets his time.

Don't get me wrong, on top of the fun experiences, I make sure that I raise him to be a respectful and responsible young man. Now that he is getting a little older, he has more responsibilities, like taking out the trash, which he sometimes fusses about, picking up after himself, etc. But I have also been teaching him how to cook, which he has a lot of interest in. I am even learning some new things while I'm teaching him. We're both enjoying this process.

When I was pregnant with my son, all I did was dance; and that is all he does now. We dance *all* the time. I have tons of videos of us singing and dancing and just having an amazing time together. Sometimes, I go into his room and watch him sleep. Mind you, he just started sleeping in his own bed. He used to sleep in the bed with me, but once he turned eleven, something switched in his head. So now I go into his room just to watch him sleep, and I pray over him and thank God for him.

I make sure that he is well affirmed and knows that he is black and he is beautiful. I give him compliments and tell him how handsome he is. He is starting to go through puberty and has breakouts from time to time, and I still let him know that he's handsome even with the acne. I need him to know when he is ready to go out into the world, that he has a strong foundation and will not just fall for anything that anybody has to say about him.

As he is maturing, he has also come into his own sense of style. When he was younger, he let me pick out his clothes, but now he is starting to have his own preferences and picks out what he desires to wear. On top of me not being able to pick out his clothes anymore, he is starting to close the door on me when he gets dressed, when he goes into the bathroom, etc. If he has boxers on, he makes sure that he has a robe on. Boy, bye! I'm your mother!

I am so blessed to have my miracle baby, but I feel kind of bad that if anything were to happen to me that King would be left to his own devices. Yeah, he has siblings on his dad's side, and plenty of cousins, but no siblings on my side. He doesn't have anybody besides me to be that shoulder that he can lean on, which tends to make me feel a little guilty at times. Would I want to have another baby? The answer that I always give is nope; I'm fine with my King but hear me out.

I had asked God if he didn't do anything else for me, could he just bless me with one child. I will do right by my child. If nothing else, just one. And God did! He blessed me abundantly. God gave me my one child and I have not had any other slip ups over the years. If there happened to be a "slip up", I would be grateful and would take the same necessary steps that I took with King.

In the meantime, I'm preparing my son to be a man in this world. He already thinks that he is the man of the house. King is always in protective mode with me. When I'm at work, he will FaceTime me and ask me if I'm okay. If I'm bringing in the groceries, he will make sure that he helps me. If we're home, he'll check on me, ask me if I need something to drink. He's just always there. That's the type of person he is.

In addition to being a protector, King is also thoughtful. Once, when he was at school, his teacher had some roses, and he asked the teacher if he could bring some home to me because I work so hard. He's even told me that when he gets older, he's going to get rich, and then he's going to take care of me and all the homeless people. He notices how much I work and even tells me to slow down sometimes or to make sure that I take a day off. Those Capricorns are something else. A good something else. King has dreams and aspirations. Even now at twelve years old, he has goals. He talks about how he wants to be independent, have his own things, and accomplish things, which I'm proud of for him to even think that way.

One thing that I'm not too proud of which I found out later when King was older, was that he would see and hear his father and I argue, and I wished he hadn't. I tried my best to protect him from our arguments, but I guess it was inevitable. I never wanted him to see me cry, so I would go and hide and shed my tears. I would get myself together before I allowed him to see me because I wanted him to always be surrounded by strong people.

King tells me that if I were to ever begin dating again, that the guy better treat me good. I believe he tells me this because of the arguments that he witnessed between his father and I. One day he asked me, "Why did you put up with that, Mom?" and "Why did you allow someone else to treat you that way, Mom?" And as much as I tried to avoid him experiencing that, the only answer that I could give was that sometimes in life you go through things. And that's the truth.

Because I am teaching my son how to be independent in this world, he is learning through me. He knows my strengths and my weaknesses and vice versa. He has witnessed my struggles with his dad and my friendships. My son knows that I am a loving, caring and a giving individual. He is the exact same way. And with him being protective of me, he will call people out when they aren't reciprocating the love.

One Christmas, because I give freely, I was dropping off gifts to various people. And this little boy asks me, "Well, what did they get you, Mom? You take care of everybody else, and you do so much for them, but I don't see anybody taking care of you, calling you, or asking you if you're okay!" Now, don't get me wrong, I do have people in my life who have showed up and showed love to us. He was just pointing out the discrepancies that he was observing.

I was baffled and amazed at the same time because I was the one that showed him that. But I had to teach him that it's not always about receiving from somebody. However, givers must set limits because takers don't have any. I found myself explaining to him that you can give and not receive, and God will bless you anyway, but realizing that I wasn't taking my own advice on setting limits with others. I ended up taking that hurt, pain, and disappointment out on my son.

King had packed up some clothes and things, some things that were even new that I had bought him. He told me that his friend didn't have any clothes and that he wanted to give them away. I noticed that he would want to give away various things and money to others, just like I did with my adopted "friends". When he would return after going out with his friends, I'd ask him, "Well, what did you do with your money?" or "How much do you have left?" And he'd say that one of his friends didn't have any money to get ice cream or a phone case or whatever. He would give his money away. I realized that he was following me in my actions as far as taking care of his friends and it was not reciprocated. And because I saw those traits in him that he had learned from me, subconsciously, I lashed out at him because I was upset with myself and the mistakes I had made with my own friendships.

The way he was managing his friendships made me confront my actions in past relationships and friendships, and how I was used, abused, and taken advantage of. So, now I try to teach him to set boundaries ahead of time. I tell him, "Don't allow people to run over you, don't let people play with you, and notice when and why people want to come around you. When people see that you are a free giver, they will take advantage of that." Because my son was behaving like me, people recognized that trait. And tried to take advantage of it. I noticed that certain friends would come around, eat up the food and the snacks, try to borrow some of his clothes, and then leave. It was something that I wanted him to be aware of. Besides, it's something that I am still learning how to do even up to this very moment.

I am, a single mother who is not only taking care of her son and herself, but I was also taking care of my mother who was laid off. I was also taking care of my father who was disabled and had diabetes. I wanted to make sure that I did right by my parents. The Bible says to honor your father and mother. So that's what I am doing; I don't want to block any blessings that God has for me. On top of that, I was taking care of other households of people that were in my circle. I felt like, since I was able to help them, I did it. But I did not realize that just because I pushed myself to be in a good position financially for my son and I, it wasn't necessarily meant for anybody else.

5 CHAPTER

Take Three

I went through a process of healing. And I knew I was healing, because there was one time, when I was cleaning my home and I found a picture of another woman that my son's father was messing around with, and you know what I did? I just gave it to him. I didn't say anything; just handed it over to him. Now if that isn't growth, I don't know what is! And do you know what he said to me? He said, "Oh, you must be mad now because she's pretty!" There were so many times where he would send me text messages that were degrading and disrespectful, where he would talk about my weight or not being attracted to me anymore; just real ignorant comments that he knew would trigger me. And all I could say was, "Wow!" This just solidified my reasoning for leaving him alone.

I took being alone literally. I didn't talk to any men. I was single, ***SINGLE.*** I remember this guy tried to talk to me while I was at the barbershop. He had his own business, plus he sold movies, CD's, and whatnot. I was getting my hair done and he was getting his haircut. He was 6'3" and dark skinned, not even my type, but he was really nice. In the mix of us sitting outside and cracking jokes, we began to have a sidebar conversation. He explained to me that he was in the midst of getting a divorce, had two kids, and he was married for about ten years. He asked me if I was married; I told him no. He asked me if I was involved, the answer was no, again. But I said that I have been through enough.

I began to elaborate on my experience with my past relationships. He told me that he could just tell from the way that I was describing my story that what I had gone through was painful. I shared with him that I didn't want to go through any more pain because enough was enough. He was very open and honest with me, which I appreciated, and told me that I seemed like a nice person and someone who he would like to get to know, but he just got out of his decade long marriage, and was ready to mingle, and he didn't want to play with me. Not just with me, but any woman. He wanted to play the field and was man enough to not take my number because he knew his motives and intentions. I ran into him a year later at the gym, and he was still playing. I was glad that he decided to not string me along because that would have been a whole year of heartache and wasted time.

During this single season, people around me would ask me if I were bitter, mad, or upset because anytime a guy would try and talk to me, I would shut it down. I was in a dark place, but I was still accomplishing some goals that I had on my list: better credit, go back to school, and just growing into a better space for myself. While we were apart, my son's father had been in multiple relationships, living with other females, the whole shebang. I was totally fine with it because I had ended the relationship; I no longer wanted it, and I was totally content with whatever he had going on while I was taking my time to heal and glow.

I would pack my son's bags and allow him to stay with his dad even when he was staying with other females. There weren't any hard feelings on my end. I was that settled with my decision. I was so settled that I didn't even give in when he would text me at five o'clock in the morning, reminiscing about us and telling me that he wanted to get back together. Nope. Didn't let it faze me. One girl even had the guts to confront me and say that my son's father believed that I was staying single for him, that I was waiting for him! Ha! So far from the truth!

There was one time when he sent me a song "You Deserve" by August Alsina:

"Girl I think it's best for me to say this, I ain't no good

And your heart ain't something I should play with

So let's get it understood

I ain't trying I just want ti make it right

And tell the judge I ain't even gotta plead my case

I can tell my baby to her face"

The song is basically saying that if I move on, that he hopes that I find better. He even got my name tatted on him, not once, but twice! As he persisted to get back with me, he called me out the blue and said, "Let's go to the Justice of Peace and get married!" But I realized that we were better off as friends. We had great times talking about different things, hanging out and just busting it up. We had become such good friends that when the time came for me to want to date someone else, I was able to talk to him about it. Not that I needed permission, but we were close friends almost.

He would apologize for his actions, but when the damage is done, it's done. I never wished ill will on him, but I was no longer in love with him. You know it’s over when you don't want to dress up for your man and look nice. You know it's over when you no longer get those butterflies in your stomach. You know it’s over when you no longer want to kiss their face, hold their hand, or just hear their voice. That is what happened to me. All I have to do was think back on all that I went through with him, and it keeps me on the straight and narrow to accomplish my goals and be prepared for someone that will treat me right.

I began to work on myself, and I also began to work on my credit. I had invested in some programs to build my score up, and during that, purchasing a car was on my goals list as well. I used to go to the “Buy here, Pay here” places, but this time around, I wanted to go to an actual dealership. I was praying to God to help me get a car because the engine was shot on my current vehicle.

I went to the dealership to see what cars they had, because listen, I was manifesting my goals. And one of the sales guys, really nice and sweet, hooked me up, and I was able to get my car! As a payback for helping me get a vehicle, I would always send people who were looking into the market to buy an automobile his way. People would give me compliments on my car and ask where I purchased it from. I would immediately let them know what kind of deal I had because the experience of getting my car was so easy. I sent over tons and tons of referrals to the sales guy. I would call him and check in to see if the customers followed through with him, plus the commission, for me and him.

Sometimes I would drop off my referrals to the dealership because they would need a ride, and I would pop my head in and say ‘Hi’ to him. Some of those times I was looking real bummy when I would show up. Bare face, no makeup, hair in a regular shmegular ponytail, looking crazy. My son’s father’s abuse still influenced me because whenever a guy was interested in me, I would always question their motives. I would always ask, “Why? Why are you attracted to me? Why do you want me?” So that mindset traveled with me while Anthony, the sales guy, and I began to become friendlier. I was so skeptical when it came to him and when it came to any guy.

Once, I had referred him to a close girlfriend of mine, Nadina, and her husband, Greg, to buy a car from Anthony. This was way before we even started getting close, but the thing is that they could already tell that there was some chemistry between us. He told them that if I ever acted up then he knew he could call Nadina to straighten me out. We were just friends, and I didn’t even like him like that, but it was nice to know that he thought of me in that way even though I wasn't really interested in a relationship at the time.

Anthony began to become more interested in me as time went on. After sending him a few customers here and there and catching a few more referral checks, we started to talk more frequently. It went from customer referrals to regular conversation. We would communicate for thirty minutes, and then it moved to sometimes two hours a night. We talked on the phone for about two years and built up our friendship. Within those two years, we became really good friends; he was an open book with me and didn't mind telling me about his life experiences.

To be honest, I didn't even like Anthony at first. I told my sister, Mona, about him and how I was helping him with referrals, and here she goes asking me if I like someone, and here I go, "No! He's corny. I don't like him!" But I still communicated and still talked to him, and he continued to reveal more about himself with me.

During the second year of our friendship, he asked me around my birthday if I had any plans because he wanted to come through and help me celebrate. But at that time, I was in a space where I felt like I needed to guard my heart. I was so used to being with one person and getting to know a new person scared me. I kept telling myself that I didn't want the same thing that happened to me in my previous relationships to happen now. I put a protective barrier around it. It was like my heart was in a boxing ring. Do not get me wrong; you should guard your heart, prepare your heart, pay attention to the red flags, but when you're already going into a relationship thinking that somebody is out to get you, that's not good. That's a sign that some more internal work needs to take place.

From the very beginning, I always questioned his motives, even during the times we talked. Like what were his real plans and intentions with me. Mind you, I was still healing, and during that journey, I realized that people can just like me for my personality. I do not always have to be all together for someone to be interested in me, which was the total opposite in my last relationships.

As we continued to talk and he continued to offer to hang out, which I did eventually, I began to open up, but not too much, just bits and pieces of my life. However, he stayed consistent with being an open book with me, which I appreciated, and was a common thread when it came to him. Anthony would reveal things that he had gone through like being incarcerated and seeing a therapist to take care of his mind, body, and soul. We were friends first before anything else.

We would talk about any and everything. Even when we would have disagreements, he would tell me that we were better than this to fuss the way that we were. There was one time when we were at odds and I had to get some more work done on my car. He offered to let me use his car, but I was stubborn. I declined his offer. Being petty. But I was really struggling with trying to figure out how I was going to get to work and back home again. I was being extra and what not. I had used his car before when things were good between us, but this time I was like NOPE! As I reflect, I could've handled our disagreements better than I did, because there were plenty of times that he was really being nice and sweet to me. If I had just communicated with him, I believe things would have turned out differently.

Quick tip for all the couples out there: Communicate with your other half. Have open and honest conversations. Have weekly check-ins with each other. Talk about what you like and don't like. Talk about something that is bothering you or that you are hurt by something. I remember him asking me what was wrong or what was annoying me. I would tell him and it would be something from the previous month. He would tell me, let's talk about it and be done with it. I've learned that once you argue about something, leave it in the past. And some things don't even need to be addressed. Just let them play out how they will, and through that some situations can be avoided and prevented.

Our friendship grew, it began to get more serious. Within about a couple months of us taking it to that next level, he started reaching his goals that were on his list which was a turn on for me. And through that, I was able to talk about my weaknesses and goals, and how I had a plan on reaching them. Anthony was an all-around great person. Great job, car, good credit, etc. He was a gentleman with manners. He had confidence and carried himself as such. He was an awesome father; I loved how he was with his kids. He was such a family man, and he loved his children. He always spoke highly about them, and that was one of things that I adored about him.

Anthony was always there for them; he wasn't missing anything when it came to his children. It didn't matter if it was early morning or late at night, he was going to be there for those babies. If he had to cancel plans to be with his children, he would do just that. He always checked in with his family members to make sure that they were good; he was an all-around family guy. Smart, intelligent, full of integrity. He was the bomb in my eyes, and I placed him on a pedestal.

There is this song by India Arie called "The Truth" that I would play whenever I was thinking about him. She sings,

"'Cause he is the truth Said he is so real.

And I love the way that he makes me feel.

And if I am a reflection of him then I must be fly 'cause

His light it shines so bright I wouldn't lie."

These lyrics described exactly how I felt about him. Anthony didn't have to do much of anything. It was just something about him; *je ne sais quoi*. It was his presence, his smile, me just being able to talk to him at any time of the day, him responding to me, etc. The times that I did spend with him, the simple things; it just felt good. I didn't need anything else. Just having him was enough.

After all the years I spent being single and trying to heal, and to end up caring for this man when I didn't even like him in the beginning, was quite different for me. Me reciprocating open and honest dialogue with another person was strange. Regardless, I vented and opened my heart to him. I was able to be bare faced, hair tied up in a pony, or freshly shampooed, conditioned and blow dried. I was able to be naked with him, not just physically, but emotionally as well. It was such a good and refreshing feeling to have.

Once, when we were having a very deep and serious conversation about being in relationships and arguments, we started talking about certain things that people may say when they're angry at their significant other because once you say it, you can't take it back. He shared with me some things that were said to him during heated arguments, and I shared the same. As soon as he heard it, he responded and said, "Oh, I would never do that. I would never say that to you." I continued to be open with him about my abusive relationships, and he asked me, "Why didn't you tell your brothers or family?" Which is a valid question. I had to explain to him that at that point in my life, I knew that I wasn't going to stop messing with him. What would be the point? We vowed that we would never say disrespectful things to each other whenever we had disagreements, to keep things on the up and up.

With us rocking heavy with each other, we spent a significant amount of time with each other. When he would stay at my house, he would make himself comfortable: drop his bag down, go in the closet and get his towel and take a shower, and just make himself at home. I would even leave him at my house while I went to work. One Christmas, we sat up, watched movies, sipped on some wine, and wrapped up gifts for our kids. For me, it wasn't about sex; it was more than that. We were very affectionate with each other. We would hug, kiss, cuddle, etc. My favorite part was playing with his beard. And that was a good feeling because for me, I had let my guard *all* the way down by this time. I had nothing to hide.

I would do little things for him while trying to take care of his heart. I knew that his favorite color was red, so I bought these really cute pajamas that said, "I '**red**' your heart" to wear for him. I would send him little cards for no reason, surprise him with lunch, send him texts or calls, pop up at his job, etc. Just to put a smile on his face. Just to show him that I was thinking about him and that he was appreciated. When I could sense it, I would send him encouraging text messages and gifts that were meant to lift his spirits. When he was feeling down again, he could always go back to that card or that text to get him back on track.

I remember being in church or Bible study and recording the sermons and sending them to him. And not that he was not spiritually connected or anything, but I just wanted to always let him know that he wasn't alone, and that if nobody else got him, me and God got him. I wanted to be there for him not just physically, but emotionally and spiritually.

I was very private with who I would tell about our friendship. I didn't want him to meet too many people that were in my life because if things didn't end up well between us, I didn't want to have to explain myself to everybody when they would ask about him. Tamika, one of my sisters, knew about Anthony, but never met him in person. Tamika, by the way is my baby. She is my personal hairstylist. We would always have sleepovers and hang out together. She was my go-to whenever I wanted to have some fun; it's always laughs and good times with her.

Once while at the mall with her, we were shopping and eating, and Anthony calls me and tells me that he was rushing and forgot his lunch because he had to go in early to meet a client. He asked me to pick him up something and drop it off. I already knew what he wanted and so I picked up his usual from his favorite spot in the mall. Now, I had no choice but for him to meet Tamika because we rode in her car together that day. I had her take me to his job and I introduced them to each other.

The Grass Isn't as Green As It Seems

One thing that I do wish that I had done was kept my guard up and acknowledged the red flags that I saw. Do you ever hope and pray that things just work out because you want them to work out that badly? You block out all the red flags, warning signs, the up and down roller coaster feelings, and lies that are told to you because you just want it to be what you have been longing for? That's where I was.

After a year, I told Anthony that I was tired, and I wanted him to find himself. I told him to move on, and he texted me and said that he wanted me to wait for him while he was getting himself together. I don't know what made me brush it off, but it was something whispering me to break things off with him. He was in the process of purchasing a house. He would send me pictures of the type of home that he was looking for, which to me, was too big just for a bachelor. He would tell me, "Oh, a grown man can have a big house. Ain't nothing wrong with that! Plus, remember, I have kids, too." On top of that, his father was sick and he wanted to make sure that he had enough space to take him and care for him.

But six months later, he had to come clean about some things that he was doing once he moved into the house. Anthony revealed that he was unable to get the title of the house in his name and was having financial issues. On top of that, he admitted that he was trying to figure out if things would work out between him and his son's mother. And I asked him why he didn't tell me this six months ago when I gave him the opportunity to leave our situation with clean hands. He told me that he didn't want to miss out on a good thing.

I was hurt by his truth. I went to see him at his mom's house, and I couldn't even look him in his face. He asked me, "Why can't you look at me?" and all I wanted to say was, "YOU'RE A LIAR!" But the only thing that could come out was, "I'm hurt." That's all I could say.

Since I immediately thought that he wasn't the kind of guy that I would have been attracted to in the past, I figured he was what I needed. Someone who was different, someone that I wouldn't have to chase down, or because he didn't catch my eye right away, I thought this would have a different outcome. I will say that I have learned that just because a man is quiet or presents himself in a certain kind of way, does not exempt him from cheating or playing women.

I looked at him differently because he presented something to me that was different from what I was used to. He was open and honest about why his relationships didn't work out or why he was cheating. I figured that this was taken care of and was in his past and not his present. He didn't put his own self on a pedestal, I did that.

After I found out about his history, and the fact those patterns were still present with him, I continued to care about him. It took about a week for me to contemplate if I was going to continue a friendship with him or not and ending up deciding that I was. At this point in time, I had already gained feelings for him and even though he lied about a lot of things and hurt me, I decided that I was going to forgive him. When feelings are involved, and you have invested those feelings, it is harder to leave. So, we moved on with a clean slate, or so I thought.

I still had a bad taste in my mouth about him lying to me. Whenever we would have an argument, I began to think he was always lying, leaving out bits and pieces of information. But to find out, he was being honest with me. And I say that because he would tell me things, I didn't think that he would need to tell me, which aided in his favor and getting back on my good side.

While I was with Anthony, I learned about myself. I had to learn how to let barriers down if I wanted to have fun. We ended up taking a trip together. It was my first trip ever that I took with a guy. Literally. We went away for the weekend, and it was so much fun. I learned more about him on a more intimate level than I had ever before, and I realized that he was goofier than I thought.

Things were going well for us for a while. Anthony would always preach about good credit and he knew that I had a good score. He also knew that I always worked overtime. I was always working to make sure that I put myself and my son in a good place. While he was working on getting his own place, he called me and told me that he may need me financially. And I was cool with it because he was my friend; he was someone that I was rocking with heavy. I didn't mind.

When I said 'yes', he took that for all that it was worth. He ended up getting his own place, and I began to spend the night over there more often. We would have the best times just laughing, cracking jokes, talking, etc. I felt like he was my safe place. While I was over at his house, we talked for over an hour and a half and I just vented to him. I shared many things with him that I had gone through. And I told him, again, that if he didn't have good intentions about being with me, then just walk away. Nobody was forcing him to stay. We were already good friends, and I didn't want to mess that up. I was willing to let him go and let him do him.

I wasn't naive about the fact that he had other friends, but I'm not sure if I just made that up in my mind. I guess I wanted it to just be us that I would ask him those questions just to check. He would never come out and say that he was messing with other women. And to his credit, he was always busy. He was always with his children or always working. I took his answers as a grain of salt.

And that grain of salt went quickly. After being in his own place for a little bit, he also asked me for another financial favor. He was trying to take a trip for his football tour and needed my assistance. I obliged because, again, this was a guy that I really cared for. While he was on the trip, some information was routed to my phone by accident. I had the receipts, literal receipts of how he was moving, and all the evidence I needed to prove his secret dealings that were occurring behind my back.

I didn't speak to him for a week. While I was trying to wrap my head around what was happening, what to do, and come to sense with my feelings, he left me five or six voicemails, plus called me back-to-back for that entire week. I was so angry that I didn't even listen to them until months later, and it seemed from what he was articulating to me was that he cared about me, which was the same thing that he was saying when we finally were able to talk through our situation.

Anthony explained to me that he was not into playing games; he wasn't out here going crazy and messing with a whole bunch of women. I had to break it down to him and let him know that I was already skeptical about this friendship because of the hurt I had already been in with my past relationships. I didn't want to endure any more hurt. He said that he wasn't even in the mental or emotional capacity to entertain multiple women. His response was always that he wasn't doing what I clearly knew he was.

So, here I go, once again, suppressing my true feelings, and continuing to have a friendship with him. From time to time, he would tell me that he wouldn't bite the hand that feeds him, that what I have done for him had not gone unnoticed. He had never met someone with such a big heart as mine, etc. I would hope that those things that he was saying were true because now, I felt as though so many people were out to get me. I hated to think that he was in that category, too.

The same way I was willing to accept his good, I was also willing to accept his bad for what it was worth. And it was simply based on my feelings for him. And the feeling was vice versa. Everybody has baggage and everybody has something that they need to improve or be healed from. He knew about what I had gone through with my son's father, he knew about my confidence, and other things that I had experienced. Just like I would not just drop him because of his struggles, he didn't drop me because of mine.

As we ended up continuing our friendship, nothing really changed from what we had. I would continue to stay over at his house. We would laugh, joke, chill, etc. While I was over there, he would let me wash my clothes over there and sometimes he would even wash and fold them for me.

Now, I'm not saying that we were boyfriend and girlfriend, we were friends, and I knew that, but I did feel like I was with All State Insurance, in good hands when it came to Anthony. He would even say, "We're better than this, Ty" when he would confess to his faults because he knew what kind of friendship we had. And that to me meant he cared about me, or at least had me thinking that way.

I didn't even tell my really good friend, Kenya, about Anthony until months later, and it wasn't even intentional. We were out getting a bite to eat and having some drinks, and he started to text me that he wanted to see me. I decided that there would be no better time than this. I mean at the end of the day; Kenya was my friend. So, I invited him to grab a drink with us and she met him for the first time.

On the drive back from dropping her off, I told her everything. I told her how he was my friend, but that we had been dealing for a little while. I even told her that we had gone on a trip. She was so shocked. She couldn't believe it.

With me trying to love Anthony from the inside out, he became the first man I had helped financially. I helped him whenever he needed me, which was often. I was hoping during me helping him, that he wasn't being frivolous with his own money knowing that I was sacrificing and helping him in his time of need. Even though I wasn't in a committed relationship with him, I still supported him. At the end of the day, he was my friend and I had feelings for him. When it seems as though someone is rocking with you the long way, you do what you can. I was there in any way, shape, or form for Anthony, but I hadn't realized how much I had really helped him until it was too late.

I had just become a licensed Zumba instructor and I was looking for a space to hold my classes. I found one that I was in love with. It wasn't too far from my job, and I had a feeling that it was going to work out for me. When I went to apply for it, I was denied. I found out that my credit score had dropped, and I immediately thought to myself, "Oh, my gosh! How?!" I couldn't figure out why this was happening. I knew I had good credit. I had already saved a few coins for the down payment. Something wasn't adding up.

To my surprise, one of my credit cards was maxed out. Another card had a balance because I was just helping, and helping, and helping, and I never checked in on it. I have this little book with a record of all the money I have lent out to people. Within the book, just for my own record keeping, nothing else, I have names of people that have asked to borrow money from me. The money could have been for anything: rent, groceries, electric, cable, etc. I decided to go through the book and just sat there and cried because I literally lent out and gave almost twenty thousand dollars to people!

Yes! You read that correctly! Twenty thousand dollars! And half of that I had given to Anthony. Ten thousand dollars lent out to one man. I never said no to him. I never took a moment to think about it. When I found out about him being in some tight spots, The Girl with The Big Heart would emerge and try to be Super Woman over and over again.

The Boy Is Mine

During my bad habit of adopting friends and lending out money, a former classmate of mine, Monica, and an associate from my clubbing days, Sharonda, and I reunited and started spending a lot of time together. It just so happened that Sharonda was related to Anthony, and Sharonda and Monica were already friends. The three of us would hang out together, go out to the bar, and chill on a weekly basis. I would invite them to my family functions where we played cards, cooked, and Monica's son and King were around the same age, so they became good friends, too.

During the family functions, I would see Monica consistently flirting with one of my family members. One thing about me is that I don't mix family and friends, because at the end of the day, if things go sour, I didn't want anybody to be mad at me or put me in any awkward situation once the dust settled. I just kept this separate to keep the peace. On top of that, as her friend, I knew who she really had feelings for, so I was protecting my family member as well.

While hanging with Sharonda and Monica, Anthony's name would come up from time to time, and when you are drinking, you can have word vomit. But I would not say anything; I would just listen. Monica would bring up Anthony's name periodically, and I started putting some things together. You know, Inspector Gadget came out again. With all the pieces in hand, I asked Monica to come over to my house, so that I could clear the air about some things.

I told her that Anthony was my friend, and even though we had just reunited after many years, I was more inclined to continue a friendship with him rather than her. She ended up telling me that it wasn't that serious and whatever they had going on was in the past. She changed the subject and proceeded to tell me about the new guy she was interested in at the moment. So again, I took it with a grain of salt, and didn't let this affect our friendship.

However, I realized that there was a conflict of interest, but I didn't end up following with my gut. My gut told me that I shouldn't continue to befriend Monica, although she was saying that it didn't matter, or that she wasn't into him anymore. I should've listened to my intuition and walked away from the friendship. I really liked Anthony, but I didn't want to cause any conflict. Unfortunately, it ended up turning sour in the end.

Throughout that year, the three of us, Monica, Sharonda, and I continued to stay acquainted with one another; however, I ended up finding out that Monica had inquired about Anthony and his relationship status. I took it upon myself to reach out once again and clarify what was really going on between them. I asked Monica if she still had feelings for him, and she boldly said that she was not too sure about how she truly felt about Anthony. Regardless of how foggy her feelings were, my feelings for him were clear, and by this time I was willing to part ways with her.

But before we did, she asked why I felt as though she wasn't good enough for the family member that she was interested in. I had to tell her straight up 'no.' 'To be honest, from the things that she would share with me as her friend, I didn't agree with how she was moving in her life. So, as far as I was concerned, no, she wasn't good enough for my family member.

After our second conversation about Anthony, nothing really changed between her and I. I even took it upon myself to help her out in her times of need. There I go adopting people, again. Shame on you, Ty! Within that year of helping her, she ended up disappearing on me, and I'm not going to lie, that hurt. She just left without any explanation. No apology. No justification. No nothing. I didn't speak about my hurt to anyone; I just kept quiet. My motto is if someone owes you, you shouldn't have to call to remind them of their debt.

A year later, Monica pops back up and she immediately needs a place to stay. I let her stay with me. Y'all know me. That's what I do. I just can't turn people away during their time of need. To be honest, I really couldn't say 'no 'because I would want someone to say 'yes 'to me if I needed the help.

When she moved in, we kind of just picked up our friendship where we had left it. We would hang out, stay up, drink our wine, talk, vent, etc. While rekindling our friendship, I had this intuition that something was going on between Monica and

Anthony, again. I did some of my Inspector Gadget work and found out that my woman's intuition was correct. I learned everything I needed to know about the situation.

I found out that they were messing around with each other behind my back, while I was helping them both financially! Hurt and shocked is an understatement. Surprisingly, Monica told me the truth. When I reached out to Anthony and asked him about what was going, no surprise there, he was honest about the fact that Monica had reached out to him first, which confirmed my evidence. But when he said he didn't entertain it because of me, I knew that was a lie. And because of that part, I had to sit back and re-evaluate, because this wasn't the first, second, third, or fourth flag I had seen from him.

I acknowledge that everybody has a past, people hit and miss each other throughout the years; it was almost like that was what was going on between them. They had been two ships passing in the night, but the door was always open. When Monica slid that door open, you could slide in, and that's exactly what Anthony did. Monica stayed somewhere else for a day or two so things could calm down between us. However, she didn't feel comfortable where she was staying, so I let her come back to my house, but I continued to distance myself from her.

When I found out about Anthony and Monica, I had a choice to make; I didn't end up making the right one. I know the part I played, and I know I should've left both of them alone. If I had left him alone and continued being friends with her, he would've stayed on my mind of what could've been, so I continued to have a friendship with both parties.

After further and deeper reflection, the main reason why I didn't really stop messing with him was because I already had feelings for him. I was surprised that I was able to care about somebody and want to love again. I was scared to feel this again, but I wasn't going to hold myself in captivity either. I know now that I still have a heart, I still have feelings because for so long, I was numb to love. Plus, the last time I had talked to Monica I was sixteen years old, still in high school. I had seen her twice before during my adult life. In my mind, I had invested more time with him than her, and I wasn't willing to let that go.

Real Love. I'm Searching for A Real Love.

After the truth revealed itself, my friendship with Anthony remained. I still had feelings for him, and what you probably already know is that feelings don't just go away like that. My feelings for him overrode the ten thousand dollars I had lent him. My feelings for him overrode the lying and the betrayal. Sometimes people think that it's all about money, and it's not. It is about principle. It is about appreciation. It is about gratitude. All of those things. Money and materialistic things come and go. Time and invested feelings, not so much.

When it comes to me and who I am romantically involved with, I am always going to ride. When it comes to their situations and their problems, they become my own situations and problems. In the beginning, I helped Anthony out of the kindness of my heart because I did care about him. At the end of the day, if I am sacrificing for you as a single mother, and I decide to help you out of the little bit that I got, and then you bend over and tell me to kiss your butt, that's when it becomes an issue.

I was more hurt at the fact that I did all of those things out of love for him, and I really had nothing to show for it. I did it out of the fact that I thought that I could be his Superwoman and take care of his heart and protect it, but little did I know that he had some internal work that needed to be taken care of first. I couldn't just knock him off his feet with my love and charm.

Have you ever loved or cared about someone so much that in the midst of you trying to understand them, they end up hurting you? It's like you try to rationalize their actions. They've been through this or that, they've experienced some kind of trauma, and you still try to deal with them, look past their flaws, or make up every excuse that you can think of to still be there? That's the kind of stuff I do. I know it hurt me. I know it's not right, but I'll still stick around.

I think I have a problem with trying to play both roles when it comes to relationships. I try to be the man and the woman. I automatically want to take care of them, cater to them, be there for them, etc. I try to keep it spicy, spontaneous, and interesting by playing both parts. With him being such an open book, I thought if I did the same thing, that he would be genuine with who he was as a person.

While trying to care for someone else's heart, I ended up hurting my own. I always say, "Don't hurt your own feelings," but sometimes when you get caught up, you end up doing the very thing that you said you wouldn't. Nobody can tell someone else how to feel or not to have feelings for someone when you have created a bond and a friendship; especially if it is going to another level.

My heart always tells me little things in big ways. I am a firm believer in the fact that hurt people hurt people. We attract what we are. If you don't love yourself, you are upset with yourself, disappointed, sometimes you deal with people that have those same issues. You think you can work with them and build something together, heal from it together, but not always. Some people also hurt you in the process of their healing.

For you to learn a lesson, sometimes it takes you being hurt hard enough to know that this isn't for you, so you won't go back. I've been hurt where I was able to say, "Okay, no. This is not for me." And I'm rather good at exiting that situation by not going back, not reaching out to that person; but if that person were to reach out to me, a feeling inside of me would rise out looking for closure.

I told you in the beginning that I share my story because maybe someone can learn from this. Writing this book has been a major tool in my healing process. I can grow and reflect from this by being able to address and discuss about my mistakes. I'm learning a lot. I can see my flaws and my mistakes. I'm able to take responsibility and accountability and say that I shouldn't have done this or that.

When I think about it, I had been in relationships before, but I wasn't in an official one with Anthony. We had no title, but I acted as if I did. I did more for him than I ever did for anybody else. Even being with my son's father for thirteen years, there were things I never did for him that I did for Anthony.

After completing some major contemplation, I realized that I needed to step away from Anthony as well, regardless of what my heart wanted. I began working on getting myself back, getting things in order for myself. During our time of distance, Anthony would reach out to me and I didn't respond because I needed to get back to Ty.

Anthony's cousin, Sharonda, and I continued our friendship after everything went down. We were already talking on the phone every day because we had the same lunch break, but our closeness intensified even more. Throughout our conversations, I ended developing a soft spot for her because she was cool, easy to talk to, and my favorite part, brutally honest. We hung out, threw barbecues, texted each other inspiration throughout the day, etc. She even shared her point of view about the situation and didn't really take sides which was understandable.

While hanging out with Sharonda at the barbecues, there would be various people who would come around, as well. And a couple of them would try and talk to me, flirt, get my number and what not. But to find out, Monica had messed with them also. Knowing me, that wasn't a line I was willing to cross regardless if her and I weren't on good terms. That's just the type of person I am. I don't hold grudges and I'm not a revengeful person.

At this point, I wish everybody the best. I've learned a major lesson because I had plenty of warnings and didn't listen to them. This is my karma and I must pay for my consequences.

6 CHAPTER

Lesson Learned

Throughout these experiences, I have learned so many things about myself that to be honest, if I had not gone through this, I might have continued this vicious and toxic cycle of helping and adopting others. Even though the lessons hurt, I'm learning and growing for the betterment of myself and my son. I'm glad that my son never suffered from the mistakes that I have made in the past. I never took anything away from his childhood or shortchanged him because God put me in a position to help others.

I make sure that I keep a smile on my face for King. I do my best to hide when I am upset so that he doesn't see me cry when I'm triggered about the past. I am always determined to make sure that I am fully present when it comes to my son. If he wants to sing and dance, I'm down. If he wants to go for a ride, let's do it. If he wants to have a pillow fight or just wants to watch TV, let's go. I am down for whatever, when it comes to him. Because at the end of the day, we are all we got!

It's Healing Time

While going through this healing journey, the main thing that I do want is total and complete healing. The last thing that I don't want to do is take my pain and hurt and lash out onto a friend or my next relationship. You know the saying, "Hurt people hurt people". And I realized that quote applies to me. To heal, I have to practice better judgement on people's character and have better discernment while choosing my relationships.

Nobody put a gun to my head and made me do this or put up with that. I allowed *a lot* of people to take advantage of me. What you allow is what's going to happen. What you settle for is what you are going to get. I must be more mindful and careful of what I settle for and what boundaries I make. If people do things to you, and you don't speak up, it's basically saying that you are accepting whatever they are dishing out to you. You are allowing them to disrespect your boundaries.

There were times when I would go to church and the minister would prophesy to me, and honest to God, I genuinely believe if I had listened to what God was trying to convey to me and took heed of the prophecy, I would have avoided a lot of pain and heartache in my life.

You know the saying, "Warning before destruction." My friend, Nadina, called me one day and told me that God had dropped something in her spirit about me. She told me that I wasn't to help anyone financially and she gave me a certain time frame as well. She warned me and said if I did help anybody, there would be consequences. And the consequences would be only of my own volition.

When God shows you something, you better believe it. I asked God to forgive me for anything that I had done willingly and unwillingly because there were things that I didn't really realize what I was doing, it was just out of habit. I also asked God to forgive me for what I tolerated and what I let happen to me. I'm in a different place in my life and on a road where I'm learning from mistakes. It's definitely hard to take responsibility for my actions, but I'm tired of beating myself up about it. I put myself in the ring, gave myself a couple jabs, and just went off. I will no longer do that.

When you are a genuine person, not perfect, but genuine, and have the right motives in what you're doing, God will still look out for you even when you aren't making the best decisions for yourself. In the situations where I couldn't leave, it always ended up where the ties were severed because I couldn't do it myself. It was like God said, "Oh since you're weak in this area, I'll end it for you." And when God does cause the separation and I cared about the person, I'll always want an explanation, not knowing that it was God the whole time.

When I was going through these situations, I didn't ask God, "Why me? Why me?" Instead, I would say, "God, help me through this. Walk me through this." because I don't want someone that needs my help to come to me and I say 'no 'because of how other people took advantage of me. I would also make sure that I was honest with God. I would tell him that I was hurting and in pain. And getting closer to God has brought me to the point I am at now in my healing process.

I make sure to try and read my Bible without beating myself up because sometimes I didn't read the entire book, or I didn't understand what I had just read. Although, I am not perfect, I stay connected. I make sure I go to church, hop on the prayer calls, listen to sermons, etc. Anything I can do to help me stay connected spiritually because I don't really know how to explain it, but I am a very spiritual person and always have been.

At some point in your life, you realize that you have certain patterns, certain behaviors. And once you identify them, you can no longer blame anybody but yourself. I recognized my behavior, which was adopting people and taking care of them. That was my issue; that was my thorn. However, it is something that I needed to work on. Instead of immediately giving a helping hand when people would come to me with their problems, I had to learn just to be a listening ear or a shoulder to cry on. I had to learn it wasn't my responsibility to bail people out if they came to me when they ran into financial hardships.

People will fall in love with your hand before they fall in love with your heart and unfortunately it took for me to learn the hard way before I truly understood this concept. I am removing myself from people who mean me no good and I am no longer feeling guilty about it. I am putting myself first, speaking up for myself, and recognizing when someone is attempting to play on my heart strings because I don't have to save everyone.

While I have been healing, I also put some goals in place to help me. I decided to get not only a Life Coach, but also a therapist. My therapist helped me unpack the pain and grief from the passing of my Aunt Channy and, the why behind this adopting syndrome. I know I have good intentions when it comes to helping other people, but I want to know why I do certain things.

Why do I want to help people so badly? Why do I help the wrong people? Why didn't I love myself? Why didn't I think I deserved better? Why didn't I give myself better? Why do I tolerate disrespect, dishonesty, and excuses when I know they are doing it? I'm not stupid. I'm not dumb or slow, but there is something within my being that will simply look past it. I had to stop saying, "Why me? Why me?" and stop putting myself in these positions in the first place. And my Life Coach assisted me in identifying toxic and unhealthy friendships and relationships, building up self-esteem, and writing this book.

I hadn't really shared my goals with anyone. I just wanted to execute them and accomplish them, and as I started working through my list of goals and checking them off, I made sure that I wasn't distracted in any way. I have even shut down my Facebook from time to time because I wanted to keep my goals in the forefront of mind.

Friends! How Many Of Us Have Them?

I have surrounded myself around many harmful friendships, but I am so grateful for the genuine friendships that I have established. The friends that were always looking out for me, good, bad, or indifferent. Chelsey, my god sister, was one of those. Even when I went through things with my son's father, I kept a lot of our problems from her because I just didn't want to hear her mouth. But after all the hiding I did, she still found out because my son's father wasn't hiding anything. He was all out in the open and just didn't care how I looked in these streets.

One time, my son's father was out with Jasmine, and Chelsey happened to see him; she asked me to come over and I did, and she was trying to prepare herself to break everything down to me, but little did she know that I already knew what he was doing. Chelsey was shocked. I am not sure if she was more shocked at the fact that I had kept it from her, or the fact that I already knew.

Chelsey was there for me during the times when I was removing myself from my son's father, and in my single season. She was there to encourage me, lift me, and to speak life into me. She told me how beautiful I was and that any guy would be lucky to have me. Even with all the support, I just wasn't ready to jump back into the pool of dating. And not because I still wanted my son's father back, but I was just trying to get to know me once again.

During the "Returning Back to Ty Project", Chelsey and I hung out a lot. She is such a great cook; she makes the best banana pudding. I would go over to her house with King, watch movies, take jello shots, cook, play games, the whole nine yards. She was just there for me and she continues to be there for me. We would butt heads with one another and had to agree to disagree when it came to whom I allowed in my life and space; but I knew that I could always count on her to be consistent with me. And when you have friends like that, you don't just give that up so easily. There was plenty of time and love invested in that friendship. And I am still learning to this day that you don't give the same benefits to new friends that you do to old friends. It must be earned.

Now, Kenya, was my friend, but she also hurt me to my core, so I learned how to keep things from her. I had vented to her about some things that I was going through, and when it was repeated, I knew that it could have only come from her. And that crushed and hurt my heart. It left such a bad taste in my mouth that for years I didn't let my emotions show or tell others how I was feeling. I could literally be sitting next to you wanting to cry or really going through something, and I wouldn't say a word.

To try and trust someone new was very far-fetched for me. Now, I'm not saying that I never opened up, but I knew exactly how far to open with certain people and what to say to whom. With that strategy, I knew who I could trust because if something was repeated, I knew exactly who it came from. I'm still like this until this very day.

One friend that I felt as though I could trust and be honest with was Donna, Ya'll remember her? I told y'all that I would swing back around and discuss her further. Donna was my son's father's cousin's girlfriend. She was an authentic and pure friend. She was someone that I could talk to without judgment, someone that I could vent to, and someone that supported me. I could always pack a bag and stay with her from time to time. We were so attached to each other that we even made a pact that we would get pregnant at the same time, which we actually did! Even after my son's father and I separated, she continued to encourage me and was always a listening ear.

Donna was a very private person, like I was. She wouldn't always speak on what she had going on. She would have small talk about how unhappy she was or how she needed some changes in her life, but she never went into details about what was really happening. Which I understood because you just cannot open up to everybody, you have to feel comfortable to do so. However, she did share with me that she wanted better and was thinking about relocating. So, we made plans for her to stay with me, work on some things together, and then maybe she would relocate. I was so excited for our new journey together.

But she just up and left; and when she left, it crushed me. I became distant; we stopped talking everyday like we used to. I became a little different because I was hurt, and I never really had the chance to explain to her how I felt. I felt like a true friend left me. And when she left, I really believe that I began to adopt people more and more because I was trying to fill the void of her. And I feel like if she hadn't left, things would not have happened the way they did. But as we know, everything happens for a reason.

The friends that I had at thirteen years old, I knew inside and out. Everybody goes through stubborn phases, different stages. I'd rather take that over the situation I put myself in, and granted, these friends that I have, I have helped too, but we had a history together. Whether I gave money, offered a shoulder, everything is mutual. I didn't have to call and say, “You owe me! Pay me back!” We had a system in place already and I wish I would've stayed inside of my circle. It's good to meet new people; different people can level you up, but that doesn’t mean to start doing the things I did before you determine if they are true friends or not.

While going through my seasons of adopting people and creating new friendships, I learned that whenever there is a group of three or four women, they can't be real friends. It seems like it is just never really too genuine. I had friends who would talk about me when I would leave, and vice versa. If you are really friends, you should be able to talk about those things to their face. I have grown to understand to not let other people talk about your friends when they are not around. However, even in my adult life this kind of stuff still happens. The thing is that people usually know all your business because you tell your friends, and they get to talking. Now don't get me wrong, it is perfectly healthy to vent; however, just be careful of who you vent to because every listening ear is not a safe space.

People become friends because of their common interests, and sometimes that common interest may be to hate somebody, or gossip, or whatever which can get you in trouble. That is when the "he said, she said" stuff happens. When things hit the fan and someone talks about you, will you still have the integrity to not repeat things that were told to you in confidence? Sometimes, it's not even called for. You can be the bigger person and just let people be. If you know someone is a liar or fake, let them live their life and continue to be fake. Even those times when you can say something, say less. Now, I'm not saying to not speak up about your hurt. Don’t let people walk all over you, but you must pick your battles.

When you're choosing your friends and you’re on the outside looking in, never compare and never become so desperate to be a part of something. Make sure that you are a part of a group of women that don’t have hidden agendas. You may see a group of women that are close and tight, and you desire that; you want to be part of a sisterhood. They may seem inspirational and motivational, but once you become infiltrated into the circle, you realize that it is not all it’s cracked up to be. Nothing but gossip and drama. When you’re considering friendships, you have to ask yourself the hard questions about who you will associate yourself with.

I made a vow to myself that for three to six months, I wasn't going to help anyone financially, and just see how much I could save and how much I could accomplish. Lending money out to various people and adopting friends has been my biggest downfall. I don’t want to block any blessings; however, I also don’t want to be clueless, naive, or dumb either. I never want to feel the way I feel now, used, and abused. I don’t want to be associated with people where I help them and then I don't hear from them again until they need something else from me. I have helped so many people, that it's starting to be difficult to differentiate who is real and who is just there for what I can do for them.

With my Life Coach, I have been working through on how to decipher between healthy and unhealthy relationships, and I am not just talking about romantic ones. I am re-evaluating who's *really* my friend and who I'm just a convenience to. The pain is necessary because I'm hard-headed. I ignored the gut feelings and red flags.

I want to be surrounded by people who I am not financially taking care of. I have always been an observer. When you're doing something for somebody and they are calling you, texting you, and telling you that they love you while you are doing things for them, I learned to watch those kinds of people question and their motives to see if they were truly genuine in their gratitude, or just using me. And in those times, where I had suspicions about this kind of shady activity, I was never wrong. I always trusted my instincts.

It's Gonna Be Me

I am currently at a place where I am learning how to be my own best friend. The other day, I had take-out and a drink. Dolo, by myself, and I just wrote in my journal. Sometimes you need that; you need that alone time to do stuff by yourself. So, take the selfie and be okay with it. You don't always have to be around people. You don't always have to be in the mix. And being by myself is all a learning process for me. Experience is a brutal teacher, but it is necessary. God will not put on you more than you can bear, and he will become the ultimate friend.

Not only was I working on being my own friend, I worked on being my own lover, as well. While going through my single season, I was having gatherings with my family and friends. We would have sleepovers together and everything. Being around people was my outlet while I was enjoying my singleness and being single felt good. It felt good to lay my head down at night and not think about if someone was cheating on me. It felt good not crying myself to sleep. It felt good not worrying about if the phone rings at two and three o'clock in the morning, wondering who it was.

I don't know what it is, but I hate starting over. I hate having to get to know someone all over again. I hate having to go through the dating phase. And I think that is one of the main reasons why I stayed in these toxic relationships for so long and tolerated so much. I got comfortable with that one person, I learned that one person, and I didn't want to have to learn somebody new. I didn't want to have sex with a new person; I just wanted to stick with whom I was with.

My mom always told me growing up, that you don't want a whole bunch of guys to say that they had you. So that has always stayed in the back of my mind. If a group of guys can sit around, laugh, and talk about how I was, then I wasn't wife material. Nobody would ever want or ever make an honest woman out of me. To avoid all of that, I would just stay and try and make it work, no matter how bad it hurt.

I pray that the next time someone comes into my life and wants to genuinely love me, care for me, appreciate me, that I won't push them away. I hope that I will be in a place to receive it because of all that I have been through in previous relationships and friendships. I don't want to think that they are just playing with me and playing on my kindness or think that they are out to get me.

I don't want to punish someone that could love me based on what somebody else has done to me in the past. I don't want someone else to pay for something that they didn't do. So that means that I really need to heal in all areas of my life, so that I can identify and recognize the true love that is for me. On top of that, the next time I meet someone, I want to wait until it is really serious before I come out in the open with my relationship. I want something that is that tight and strong, so there won't be anything that could keep us apart.

Which leads me to not being desperate to be in a relationship. When you are on the outside looking in, don't always assume. You make an ass out of yourself when you assume. Sometimes, social media will paint this pretty picture of a couple's relationship and start thinking that they are #relationshipgoals. But you cannot jump to conclusions that they have it all together and start comparing your own life to the internet.

There were married people that I knew, who on the outside looking in, seemed as though they had everything together; it was picture perfect. But on the inside, the couple wasn't happy, one was stepping out on the other, crying themselves to sleep, and staying because of the longevity of the relationship or kids, etc. That goes to show that marriage doesn't always equate to happiness and singleness doesn't always equate to being miserable. It's not all what it is cracked up to be. And you've done all this comparing and beating your own self up for no reason.

Although, I was hurt, manipulated, and sometimes marriage and relationships don't seem to be all that they are cracked up to be, this doesn't mean I won't try again. As well as I am doing by being single, I am not going to allow my past experiences to dictate how I move in the future. I know one day; I will truly be blessed. I know that I will find good friends. I will find a good man. And when I mean find, I am going to allow some things to pursue me rather than the other way around, so it can be right and feel right.

It's Only The Beginning

I pray and hope that my story has touched you in some way. I pray that it has encouraged you to do a deep reflection on your friendships, relationships, and self-worth. Just because you might have gone days, months, or even years of allowing people to exploit you, like I did, doesn't mean that you can't start again. This is not the end, but let me tell you, it is only the beginning.

To help you on your new journey, keep this advice in mind:

- Welcome the uncomfortably as you start a new chapter in your story.
- Show up for yourself, first. If you continue to pour into others, but not yourself, you will always be empty.
- Just because you do something for somebody, does not mean that they have to appreciate it, thank you for it, love you like you do, do the same thing for you, they don't have to show up like you showed up, etc. They don't have to do any of it. That's why you must have boundaries.
- You can't love someone into loving you.
- Nobody owes you anything.

- You don’t have to stay up to date with those who aren’t for you. Keep it in the past

- Don't have expectations of people. Do not put people on pedestals. Do not put people so high because we are all humans.

- Loneliness and unhealthy attachments will have you accepting less than what you deserve.

- Heal, and heal properly before getting with someone else.

- Do not let anything drain you, distract you, and don't be bitter about anything. When you walk around with animosity, it drains you. It's taking away your energy and your vibes. Stay positive.

- Do not ignore the red flags.

- Forgive those that hurt you.

Finally, everything that has happened before you or to you was all for a purpose. Every single betrayal. Every single lie. Every single disappointment. Was all for a reason. How do I know? Because if it wasn’t all for my pain being for a greater good, a greater purpose, I wouldn’t have been able to get to this point. I wouldn’t have been able to see the other side of the pain. When you get there, protect it. The light and energy that I am literally experiencing right now, I am protecting at all costs. The healing that it is taking place. The moves that are taking place. The positivity and love that are taking place. Trust me when I say, I am never leaving.

I love it here.

See you on the other side.

ABOUT THE AUTHOR

Author Ty Redden, is a single mother born in Wilmington, Delaware. They Lost More Than They Took, is her first book based on her life experiences. She's been working in the medical field since 2005. She loves singing dancing and socialize with friends and family.

Ty's very transparent and open with her story with hopes that her story will encourage others to set boundaries and think through life decisions and create better outcomes for themselves.

Last but not least that no one is perfect we will all make mistakes we must learn from them, so we don't repeat the same cycles.

~Ty Redden

www.ingramcontent.com/pod-product-compliance
Lightning Source LLC
LaVergne TN
LVHW020643100826
845148LV00012B/2319

* 9 7 8 1 7 3 6 8 7 8 8 2 8 *